The Archived Web

Books by Niels Brügger

Internet Histories (Ed. with G. Goggin, I. Milligan, V. Schafer). London: Routledge, 2018.

Web 25: Histories from the First 25 Years of the World Wide Web (Ed.). New York: Peter Lang, 2017.

The Web as History: Using Web Archives to Understand the Past and the Present (Ed. with Ralph Schroeder). London: UCL Press, 2017.

Histories of Public Service Broadcasters on the Web (Ed. with M. Burns). New York: Peter Lang, 2012.

Web History (Ed.). New York: Peter Lang, 2010.

Strukturalismus (with O. Vigsø). Munich: Wilhelm Fink Verlag, 2008.

Archiving Websites: General Considerations and Strategies. Aarhus: Centre for Internet Studies, 2005.

Media History: Theories, Methods, Analysis (Ed. with S. Kolstrup). Aarhus: Aarhus University Press, 2002.

Lyotard, les déplacements philosophiques (Ed. with F. Frandsen, D. Pirotte). Brussels: De Boeck-Wesmael (Le point philosophique), 1993.

The Archived Web

Doing History in the Digital Age

Niels Brügger

The MIT Press
Cambridge, Massachusetts
London, England

This book was published with support from Aarhus University Research Foundation.

This book was set in ITC Stone Serif Std by Toppan Best-set Premedia Limited.

Library of Congress Cataloging-in-Publication Data is available.

ISBN: 978-0-262-03902-4 (hardcover)
ISBN: 978-0-262-54971-4 (paperback)

For my mother

Contents

Acknowledgments   ix

Introduction   1
1   Doing Web History in the Digital Age   11
2   The Digital and the Web   17
3   Five Analytical Web Strata   31
4   Cases of Web History   41
5   Archiving the Web   73
6   The Web of the Past—Where to Find What?   91
7   The Web of the Past as a Historical Source   103
8   Scholarly Use of the Archived Web   119
9   Toward a Source Criticism of the Archived Web   137
10   On the Edge of the Web   149
11   Conclusion—the Future of Web History   155

Notes   161
References   169
Index   181

Acknowledgments

In a way, I started writing this book almost two decades ago, just after the turn of the millennium, when I first realized that my object of study—the online web—was disappearing before my very eyes. This discovery started a journey where some of the most important stopovers were my own experience with small-scale web archiving, my involvement in the preliminary work that eventually became the national Danish web archive, Netarkivet, a number of publications about web history, and the outlining of theoretical and methodological frameworks to help us understand the archived web.

On my journey I have met many people who have influenced the thoughts coming together for the first time in this book: my good friend and former colleague, Niels Ole Finnemann, now a professor at the University of Copenhagen, who was the number one cause of my moving from French philosophy to media and internet studies, and who has influenced my thinking on the internet and its history; colleagues in my department at Aarhus University, who have had to listen to me speak about web archives at length, without looking as though they were bored; the staff at Netarkivet, established in 2005 by the State Library in Aarhus and the Royal Library in Copenhagen, including management, IT specialists, curators, and researchers; what it is now fair to consider the international web history community, including the many contributors to the books and special issues of journals I have edited since 2010, as well as participants in conferences (the two RESAW conferences and others); the Oxford Internet Institute for hosting me as an Academic Visitor when I started writing this book in 2016, and its scholars, who asked intriguing questions when the book was only a PowerPoint presentation. You have all contributed to this book, for which I owe you thanks.

I also owe many thanks to Gita Devi Manaktala, the editorial director at MIT Press, for having taken the time to listen to my brief pitch of the idea for this book at the ICA Conference in Puerto Rico in 2015, even without having seen anything in writing. Reviewers and colleagues have also taken the time to read earlier drafts of the book and have offered invaluable criticism, suggestions for improvement, and possible references to include. In particular, I have appreciated the constructive comments from the reviewers of the book proposal and of the first draft of the manuscript, as well as from Ian Milligan, University of Waterloo, Helle Strandgaard Jensen, Aarhus University, Jane Winters, University of London, and Peter Webster, Webster Research & Consulting. Finally, I also thank the Aarhus University Research Foundation for their support.

Despite all the invaluable contributions and all the help I have received from individuals and institutions I have met in the expanding landscape of web history, the responsibility for the book's content is solely mine.

As this book traces a long journey with the archived web, it draws on insights from a number of published books, articles, and book chapters from 2000 onward. However, despite the inevitable traces of thoughts and ideas put forward in previously published material, it is completely new and follows its own line of argument.

Finally, I want to thank my wife, Jane, for having been more patient with me than I could ever have dreamt of, and for supporting me wholeheartedly—thanks.

Højbjerg, January 2018

A source can be a thousand things.

—J. H. Arnold, *History: A Very Short Introduction* (2000, p. 61)

Introduction

In the fall of 2016, Donald Trump was elected president of the United States. Over two months later, on January 20, 2017, when Trump was inaugurated, the official website of the White House—whitehouse.gov—was substantially altered, and in particular, the deletion of former President Barack Obama's web pages about climate change caused some turmoil and debate in mainstream and tech media, and on social media in general. In a relatively neutral tone, the *Washington Post* reported:

The energy page on the new White House website ... also appeared to remove any reference to combating climate change, a topic that had been featured prominently on the White House site under President Barack Obama. The page that once detailed the potential consequences of climate change and the Obama administration's efforts to address it vanished on Friday just as President Trump was sworn in. It now redirected to a broken link: "The requested page '/energy/climate-change' could not be found." In its place, listed among the top issues of the Trump administration, was a page entitled, "An America First Energy Plan." (Mufson & Dennis, 2017)

Under the heading "The Official White House Website Has Dropped Any Mention of Climate Change," the tech magazine *TechCrunch* expressed its concern more bluntly:

Trump's administration is acting quickly to dangerously reimagine reality. It has deleted all specific mentions of "climate change" and "global warming," as well as removed an entire page dedicated to the subject at the http://www.whitehouse.gov/energy/climate-change URL, which is no longer an active link. (Etherington, 2017)

However, it is usual for a new president to make fundamental changes to whitehouse.gov—including deleting web pages—when taking office. When Bill Clinton and George Bush were presidents, top political priorities were not highlighted in a list on the front page of whitehouse.gov as they later were, but in the transition from Bill Clinton to George Bush in 2001, "the first presidential transition of the Web age" (Wiggins, 2001, p. 1), white-house.gov was entirely redesigned. When Barack Obama succeeded George Bush in 2009, topics such as "Afghanistan" and "Africa" were replaced by "Taxes" and "Women," whereas "Energy and Environment" and "Health Care" remained on the website.[1] In fact, such changes are consistent with the original idea behind whitehouse.gov, as stated by the website's founder, David Lytel: "George W. Bush is entitled to use whitehouse.gov to present his own policies and views to the nation and the world" (Wiggins, 2001, p. 4). A president may himself delete content on whitehouse.gov because it is inconvenient in some way. In May 1996 the Clinton administration took down a searchable collection of Clinton's speeches, for fear that this easily accessible resource would make it easier for the Republican opposition to identify points of attack (the speech collection was later restored; cf. Wiggins, 1996).

Although the removal of web pages related to climate change from whitehouse.gov was to be expected, there are cases of web content being deleted for various other reasons, sometimes with the hope of this going unnoticed. For instance, in 2013, news media reported that the British Conservative Party had deleted more than a decade's worth of political speeches from its website, some of which might not have been in line with the party's current politics, and in 2014, during the war between Russians and Ukrainians, when a Dutch civilian airplane was shot down, a social media post by a Russian who claimed to have shot down a Ukrainian military plane was deleted.[2]

The foregoing incidents tell important stories about our culture, and about the web and its past. The first thing we learn is that since the mid-1990s, the web has been an inherent part of political, cultural, and social life in many countries, and therefore it will become an invaluable source for inclusion in studies of our culture in the future. Second, these stories attest to the fact that the online web is volatile, subject to deletions or changes that may occur at an unprecedented scale and pace, compared to those in other known media types. Third, it is evident that the online web is not an archive itself, although it may appear to be at first glance; on the contrary, someone—an individual, a group, or an institution—has to collect and preserve it and make it available.

The foregoing stories also remind us that the fundamental concern at stake here is not primarily who did what with the content on the web in the past, but rather, that we are able to document what happened, because someone has preserved the web content before it was changed or removed. In brief: someone has archived the web. In all the cases above it has been possible to evaluate the changes in detail only because the web of the past was preserved by a web archive and made available to the public.[3] These lessons are particularly important to keep in mind for future historians or academics who wish to write the history of our culture, as in many cases, since 1995, the web has been an important source to include, and in a growing number of cases the web will be the only existing source, because the activity being studied has taken place only on the web. Therefore, it is reasonable to maintain that if future historians want to build on this source type, it must be archived, so as to be available to future historians. But since the archived web is in many ways fundamentally different from other digital sources, such as digitized documents, print and audiovisual media, and even online media, historians have to become familiar with this type of source, its characteristics, and how these characteristics impact its scholarly use.

Theorizing the Archived Web

This book offers a theoretical and methodological framework for working with the archived web. It investigates some of the fundamental methodological questions related to using the archived web as a source in historical studies. The archived web is part of a larger digital media ecology consisting of digitized and online digital media forms, but it is also distinct from these. The theoretical framework may help map the digital media landscape and identify the archived web's distinctive features in this landscape, and with this as a stepping-stone, show how these features impact the use of the archived web as a source in academic research.

The aim of this book is to contribute to a critical discussion of the foundations of doing web history in the digital age—critical in the sense that the conditions of possibility, as well as the reach and limits of the use of the archived web as a historical source, are investigated. Therefore, although this book presents general theoretical and philosophical reflections about the archived web alongside some practical and concrete guidance, the overall tone of the book is closer to being theoretical rather than practical.

It should be noted that many of the insights in this book will also be relevant to scholars studying the current web. Studies of the online web have to be documented before, during, or after the analysis, to provide a stable object of study and to enable peers to examine the results. Therefore, the question of archiving the web is at the core of any academic study of the web.

In summary, this book contributes to the growing academic literature about the archived web by offering the first book-length theoretical and methodological framework to support the scholarly use of the archived web as a source. To fully understand the nature and possible uses of the archived web, the book uncovers the preconditions of the web of the past that today's scholars may study. This includes first acknowledging that the web in its online and archived forms must be considered in terms of its most basic nature, namely that it is digital, and second that what happens between the time the web is online until it appears in a web collection, ready for use by scholars, has to be meticulously investigated.

As may be evident from the substantial body of works cited, this book developed in a fruitful dialogue with the existing literature about "digital history," and with the emerging literature about web history, which comprise theoretical, methodological, and empirical studies. This also includes a number of my own books, articles, and book chapters that have been published since 2000, because they are now part of the literature. However, the book presents a large number of new insights; where it builds on parts of previously published material, the material has been reevaluated, reinterpreted, and expanded to fit the overall argument of this book.

Web History

By way of introduction it should be noted that the web is not the internet, although the two are interrelated. The internet is a network of computer networks and on this network the World Wide Web—or just "the web"—is a specific software system based on a set of rules for communicating between computers, for retrieving files, and for translating the content of the files into something that may be viewed in a web browser (that is, the HTTP protocol, the URL resource locator, and the HTML markup language, including their historical transformations).[4]

The birth of the web cannot be assigned a fixed date but to a period of time (Brügger, 2016b); nevertheless, the web has been here for at least 25 years, and therefore an interest in web history has been slowly emerging within the last few years. As Winters notes, "For contemporary historians at least, this is beginning to look like a reasonable chronological span" (Winters, 2017b, p. 239).

Web history may be understood in two partly overlapping ways. It may mean doing the history of some topic, with the web as one source among several, and it may mean writing the history of the web, based on different sources, including the archived web. In short, web history may be either history *with* the web, or the history *of* the web. For instance, the white-house.gov website may be used as a source in a historical study of government practices or interactions with the public (history with the web), or it may be used as a source in a study of the website itself (history of the web).

The point of view of this book is that of the historian or any researcher with a historical interest who wants to do web history, in both senses of the word, and who wants to use the archived web as a source but has no particular knowledge of the web, either in its online or archived form. To guide this researcher, a first step is to situate web history within the broader field of digital history, and to highlight how web history is distinct from other ways of combining digital and historical research.

Before we can dig deeper into what characterizes the archived web, it is necessary to take a couple of steps back. A better theoretical understanding of the archived web's specific characteristics must start with reflections on how the digital, as such, may be understood. It is argued that all digital media come with their own digitality—that is, a specific way of being digital. Digitality means the ways that a given digital medium is constituted as a media artifact and as a textual phenomenon, in the broad sense of the word *textual*. This means that just because digital media are digital, they are not necessarily digital in the same way; each has a specific digitality. With this insight as a starting point, it may be argued that digital media may be grouped under three major headings, depending on their provenance—that is, on how they became digital. These headings include digitized media (nondigital media that have been digitized), born-digital media (media that have not existed in any form other than digital), and reborn digital media (born-digital media that have been collected and preserved, and that have been changed during this process).

The archived web is a reborn digital medium, and as such it comes with a digitality of its own distinct from that of digitized collections and of the online web; it is important to understand this, because it establishes the array of possible ways of interacting with it. But since the archived web is a transformation of the online web, it is important to first apply the concept of digitality to take a closer look at the online web's digitality. The online web has three characteristics: it has two layers of text (what is seen on the screen, and what is hidden in the code and as attached files), it is composed of fragments (within the individual HTML file, and in the form of associated files), and it is hyperlinked (either the user deliberately activates a hyperlink, or web content is retrieved without direct user activity). All three characteristics of the online web's digitality have an impact on how the web may be archived and later used as a historical source.

Finally, to complete the theoretical framework, an analytical grid is needed to help systematically grasp the web as an object of study, because the web does not come with clear and obvious demarcations indicating how a study of it should be focused. The proposed analytical grid distinguishes five analytical web strata: the web element, the web page, the website, the web sphere, and the web as a whole. Each of these strata may be approached by focusing either on the visible side—for instance, the web element of a photograph as seen on a web page—or on the hidden side, the piece of code that produces both the photograph and the image file.

The foregoing sets the stage for establishing a deeper understanding of the digitality of the archived web. However, before setting out to investigate the characteristics of the archived web, and how these impact its scholarly use, it is important to get an overview of typical examples of existing web history, since this will help fuel a discussion of the archived web's digitality.

To understand the archived web, a good starting point is to investigate how the online web became the archived web—that is, how it was collected and preserved. The reason for this is that the archiving forms and strategies utilized in the collection phase are pivotal to all the following phases of the life cycle of the archived web, from how it may be preserved and made accessible, to how it may potentially be used for research. It is important to bear in mind that the online web is changed when archived, hence the term *reborn*. And this is not only the case at the time of archiving, it also applies to the phases of preserving and making available. Thus, it is argued that the transformation of the online web to the web in a web collection that a researcher sets out to use as a research object is constituted by three interdependent constructions, one in each of the phases just mentioned (collection, preservation, making available).

It is possible to identify a couple of characteristics of the archived web: first, a set of general challenges that exist independently of the archiving form and strategy used to archive it; second, a range of specific challenges that depend on the archiving form and strategy used. To better convey the digitality of the archived web, it is contrasted with a digitized collection and with the online web throughout this book.

Once the digitality of the archived web is established, the way its digitality affects the research process may be examined, from searching and selecting material to creating a corpus to study. This includes reflection on how the various forms of the archived web challenge the researcher's interaction with it as a source, and also on how it opens up a range of possibilities. When the researcher has become familiar with the web collection to be used, it is time to interact more concretely with the material. Therefore, I present reflections on how traditional historiographic methods may be reinterpreted and translated to fit the archived web, focusing on provenance, creating an overview of the archived material, evaluating versions, and referencing the material.

As the web does not develop in a vacuum, it is worth briefly focusing on some of the digital media that may be found on the edges of the web—that is, preweb applications and platforms that have affected, and been affected by, the history of the web, such as email, newsgroups, online chat, social media, and mobile platforms.

Parentheses

This book's approach has some implications for what is included and what is not. The focus is on web history and the archived web, and therefore the online web as such is not the topic of the book. But since the archived web is a transformation of the online web, it is important to have the necessary knowledge about what characterizes the online web, and so an understanding of the online web is a prerequisite.

Many studies of the web are about its use and users. In contrast, this book retains a clear focus on the archived web as a semiotic, textual system that the users could use in the past. Knowledge about the digitality of the web of the past in its archived form is considered an essential requirement for any study of yesterday's web use and users, since we must know what existed before examining how it was used.

Historical work should adopt a broad perspective. This means situating the history of the web, for instance, in a cultural, social, political, techno-logical, or other context—which context may vary, depending on research questions, theories, methods, and epistemology. This book acknowledges the importance of situating web history and the archived web within a broader horizon of understanding, while still arguing that knowledge about the archived web's characteristics and possible use as a source is a precondi-tion for placing the web of the past in a context, such as those mentioned above.

Historiography proper includes a variety of different source types to interpret and understand the past. This book focuses on one source type only, the archived web, since it is distinctive compared to other sources, nondigital as well as digital. But it is likely to be one of several sources in many web history studies, and it may also be integrated with other digital source types. Therefore it is pivotal to provide insights into the archived web as a source in its own right.

In contrast to methodological how-to texts that address the archived web, this is not a practical how-to book aimed at introducing specific archiving tools, web collections, and digital analysis software packages, as archiving tools, web collections, and analytical software tend to be very short-lived, and therefore this book would risk quickly being out of date. I adopt a more general and theoretical approach, discussing types of archiving forms, web collections, and analytical approaches.

However, all the above-mentioned topics are not forgotten here; they are just placed in parentheses to keep a clear focus. It is up to the read-ers, in future studies, to establish fruitful interactions between this book's insights into the archived web and the things put in parentheses. Studies of the archived web should be brought into dialogue with studies of the online web, the use and users of the past web should be brought back on stage, the archived web should be reembedded in the necessary contexts, it should interact with a great variety of other source types, and the theo-retical and methodological reflections should be translated into concrete practical guidance.

Structure of This Book

Chapter 1 situates web history—history with and history of the web—within the broader field of digital history. It highlights the importance of acknowledging that more and more historical sources come in digital form only, and that this should prompt historiographic researchers to reconsider their theories and methods to bring them into line with this new source environment.

Chapter 2 begins the theoretical and methodological work by building up from the fundamental level of what may be understood by "digital," and by introducing the concept of digitality—that is, the specific way a given digital medium embeds the digital alphabet in a material artifact and in textual systems. This chapter also presents the distinctions among digitized, born-digital, and reborn digital material alongside the specific digitality of the online web.

To complete the theoretical basis for the methodological reflections on the use of the archived web as a source in the rest of the book, chapter 3 introduces the analytical grid. The researcher may use this grid when studying the web, focusing on the web element, the web page, the website, the web sphere, or the web as a whole.

Chapter 4 provides a variety of illustrative cases of web history (in both senses of the term), drawn from the last 15 years of web history studies. Each case is a typical example of how the writing of web history has been conducted, and how web historiography questions have been addressed by existing web history studies.

Chapter 5 takes the point of view of the archiving actor—that is, the individual or organization who assumes the task of preserving the web. The chapter begins by asking why it is necessary to archive the online web, considers whether a web archive is, in fact, an archive, and introduces a broad definition of web archiving. The major forms and strategies used when collecting and preserving the web, and the challenges related to web archiving, are presented.

Chapter 6 assumes the point of view of the researcher who wants to study the archived web preserved by an archiving actor in the past, and therefore the chapter provides an overview of the major types of collections, where to look for the web of the past, and what one may expect to find in each case.

Chapter 7 takes the researcher to the next step in the research process, by looking more closely at how the web of the past presents itself as an object of study in the different types of web collections, including mapping the major challenges posed by the different digitalities of the archived web when the researcher wants to access the material.

Chapter 8 considers how a scholar may use the archived web in research projects, by reintroducing the five web strata, with a view to discussing the challenges and possibilities that the scholar encounters when seeking to study the archived web on each of the strata by the use of the different types of collections.

Chapter 9 adopts a more concrete approach by introducing how the digitality of the archived web impacts some of the practical concerns related to web history research. Before this, the chapter discusses the emerging field of collaboration between web archives and researcher communities that is an effect of the digitality of the archived web.

Chapter 10 debates the intersections between web history and the history of other digital media, and presents some of the challenges that future web history faces because of a lack of digital sources.

Finally, the conclusion presents the main insights of the book, and outlines some possible items to put on a future web history research agenda.

1 Doing Web History in the Digital Age

The digital computer and computer networks have been used by historians for decades (Thomas, 2004), but it was not until the early 1990s that the interplay between historical research and computers started to become more widespread, and it has continued to expand since then (Hockey, 2004). There are at least two partly interrelated reasons for this expansion. First, more and more source material has become digital, mainly because of digitization, which creates the possibility of including digital source material in historical studies. Second, the advent and growth of the web have created new ways of making digitized collections available, of disseminating results, and of interacting with academic peers and a broader public. One of the earliest works of historical scholarship published on the web was Edward L. Ayer's "Valley of the Shadow Project," about two communities in the American Civil War (Thomas, 2004, pp. 62–63). However, the interrelations among digital history, what is termed the "history web," and web history need to be examined in greater detail.

1.1 Digital History

The growing digitization of nondigital collections of documents and other sources, combined with the rapid spread of the web in the mid-1990s, provided historians with new ways of accessing, searching, and analyzing source material, and of disseminating the results of their studies. The latest stage of a long tradition of historians using computers is often located under the umbrella term *digital history*.[1] In an online debate in 2008, hosted by the *Journal of American History* (reported in an edited version in Cohen et al., 2008), the journal starts by defining this term: "For a start, we might define digital history as anything (research method, journal article, monograph, blog, classroom exercise) that uses digital technologies in creating, enhancing, or distributing historical research and scholarship" (Cohen et al., 2008, p. 453).

This initial definition is followed by a lively discussion about what could be regarded as "digital history," but it is striking that by and large, "digital history" is mainly concerned with how historians can improve their historical research—that is, how the use of digital media and digital networks may make historians "do our work as historians better," as Daniel J. Cohen and Roy Rosenzweig put it two years earlier, in their book *Digital History: A Guide to Gathering, Preserving, and Presenting the Past on the Web* (Cohen & Rosenzweig, 2006, p. 3). By and large, this improvement takes two directions. On the one hand, traditional sources may be supplemented by digital collections and by integrating digital analytical tools, to allow for types of studies not possible before—for instance, based on search queries in large amounts of digital material. On the other hand, digital means of communication are introduced to assist collaboration among historians, in teaching, and to support the dissemination of research results in a more fruitful and efficient way by the use of websites, wikis, blogs and timelines, or virtual exhibits, and the like.

Historians' growing interest in embracing the digital realm has involved only minimal attention to the content on computers, and in computer networks such as the internet, as something that could constitute a historical source in its own right. To a large extent, debates in historiography have focused on how the digital computer could support the research process, whereas less attention has been paid to the fundamental changes in the source material itself that the growing amount of digital content might bring about. A few figures about the amount of stored data will illustrate this growth of digital material. In 2000, 75% of all data stored worldwide was nondigital (paper, film, photographs, disks, cassette tapes, etc.), but in 2007, this had shrunk to 7%, and by 2012, to 2%. Also, by 2013 the volume of digital data was doubling a little more than every third year, whereas nondigital data hardly grew at all (Mayer-Schönberger & Cukier, 2013, pp. 8–9). This explosive growth has at least three feeder lines. First, nondigital material is being digitized; second, born-digital media, including social media, is expanding; and third, the born-digital media are being collected and preserved in various archives, including web archives. Of these three types of digital material, the born-digital grows most and fastest, and by extension, so do the collections of this type of material, insofar as it is archived. Although the figures above may be questioned, the simultaneous growth of digitized, born-digital, and reborn digital material (see section 2.1) has contributed to the last decade's explosion of the digital, which has come at the expense of the nondigital.

The effect of the major shift just described on historical research remains to be seen, since little attention has been paid to the methodological challenges that may be posed by the use of born- and reborn digital sources in particular. Since digitized sources tend to resemble the nondigital counterparts from which they derive, they have mainly been taken for granted in the same way their nondigital forms have been, often just adding enhanced searching and filtering. However, the sources that were born digital, such as websites and social media, have rarely been used, although this is slowly beginning to change.

There are well-known exceptions to this lack of attention paid to the new digital source landscape, one of the most influential being Jo Guldi and David Armitage's book, *The History Manifesto* (Guldi & Armitage, 2014), which rapidly became the subject of intense discussion.[2] Taking Fernand Braudel's idea of *la longue durée* as their point of departure, Guldi and Armitage argue that historiography should focus more on a new *longue durée* characterized by "the abounding sources of big data available in our time— data ecological, governmental, economic, and cultural in nature, much of it newly available to the lens of digital analysis" (Guldi & Armitage, 2014, p. 9). But what may be most important is not only the growing amount of data, but the form in which the data are available, namely, that they are digital. Big data have always existed, but big digital data is new. However, that the number of digital sources is growing rapidly, while the body of nondigital material is stagnating, does not necessarily imply that big digital data have to be studied as big data; studying them as "small data" may be just as relevant (see also Rogers, 2013, p. 204). Thus, the major shift is not from "small data" to "big data," but from nondigital to digital data.

If we acknowledge that historical research is now facing a major qualitative as well as quantitative shift in the source material—the shift from nondigital to digital media, and the growth of digital material—historians are probably on the threshold of an era where digital history is no longer an additional choice, but a state of affairs where opting out becomes gradually more difficult. This pushes historiography to reevaluate, and possibly rethink, its methods, and to take stock of the possible impact of the digital source landscape on historiography. As Milligan remarked, "Digital sources necessitate a rethinking of the historian's toolkit" (Milligan, 2012, p. 23).

The general questions and issues that have always been part of historiography tend to remain the same (cf. Arnold, 2000; Tosh, 2006). This includes questions about the interpretation of source material, periodization, and theories of history that persist today, and questions related to how, where, and in what condition sources were found, the extent to which they are valid and representative, whether they may be considered primary or secondary, and how the choice of sources will affect the histories that may be written. In that sense, doing digital history is no different from any other kind of historical study. What has changed, however, are the possible answers to these questions and concerns—answers that, to a certain extent, are enforced by the becoming-digital of the source material, and by the lack of obviousness concerning how it should be used. And it is important to debate these new answers, because after all, the sources and methods used to approach them provide the foundation for the next steps in the process of history writing, these being all the elements included in the interpretation of the past. Thus, a fundamental change in the source foundation comes with new challenges and new options for selection, analysis, and dissemination.

1.2   History Web vs. Web History

One of the main conditions for the expansion of digital history is the advent and rapid spread of the web since the early 1990s, but it is worth reflecting a bit more on how the possible use of the web—and not digital media in general—has been understood in the field of digital history.

An early example of how historians could use the web in historiography is the article "Historians and the Web: A Beginner's Guide" (McMichael et al., 1996). This article constitutes a sort of "roadmap" to where historians may find historical sources and results of digital research projects on the web, and it gives a set of guidelines for navigating this new landscape, for instance by the use of search engines. Although this is in the very early days of the history of the web and its use within history—for example, the authors include an entire section on slow modems as a serious obstacle to using the web—this article captures what was for many years the most widely held view of the web: it was considered either a repository for digitized sources or a medium for collaboration, teaching, or dissemination of results.

Ten years after McMichael et al. published their work, Daniel J. Cohen and Roy Rosenzweig published the above-mentioned book, *Digital History* (Cohen & Rosenzweig, 2006). As the subtitle indicates—*A Guide to Gathering, Preserving, and Presenting the Past on the Web*—they consider the web mainly a platform to help historians find, search, collect, and preserve source collections, and to present the results of their studies on websites in more interactive and multimodal ways than in print media. To capture this idea of the web as a historiographic tool, Cohen and Rosenzweig use the phrase "history web" (Cohen & Rosenzweig, 2006, p. 13), and it is the "history web" that is center stage for digital history. Thus, the web is not considered an object of study or a valuable and valid source for contemporary history, and so with few exceptions, no methodological reflections are presented concerning the status, archiving, and subsequent use of this source.[3]

In contrast to the "history web," in this book what is termed "web history" takes the idea that the web of the past itself is worthy of being studied as its point of departure. As briefly outlined in the introduction, this may be done in two different ways. On the one hand, the web of the past may be used as a historical source in a study of something other than the web—for instance, a study of collective memory related to North African immigration between 2000 and 2013, based on interviews and archived websites (Gebeil, 2015b). On the other hand, one may study the web as such, either based only on sources other than the archived web, like the history of national public service broadcasters on the web, based on policy papers, reports, and correspondence (cf. Burns & Brügger, 2012), or the investigation could include the archived web as a source, together with interviews and surveys, as seen in a study of the web in the American political campaigns of 2000, 2002, and 2004 (Foot & Schneider, 2006).[4] Hence the idea of web history understood as history *with* the web, as opposed to history *of* the web. And in those cases where the archived web is used as a source, it is just added to the broad spectrum of other historical sources, and therefore it may be used in any sort of historical study where it is relevant.

As will be shown in the remainder of this book, the web of the past, in the form of the archived web passed down to the historian, is in many ways a type of source that is very distinct from digitized collections and from born-digital material. One of the main reasons for this is the dual nature of the web, both online and archived (see section 2.2). The web is born with two textual layers, the layer visible on the screen, and the code and content of the underlying HTML file, and therefore the web may be collected, preserved, and made available to the researcher either as something looking very much like the online web or as computer code (cf. section 5.3). Each of these two forms of the archived web allows for a distinct approach to the material. In the first case, the archived web may be analyzed similarly to how sources in other media types (parchment, paper, etc.) have been analyzed, but in the latter case, where the code is available, this offers access to a vast range of computer-supported and (semi)automated methods. Thus, in itself the archived web need not be approached by means of automated methods, but it may be, if archived in a form that enables this. Therefore, as maintained in section 5.3, when characterizing the archived web it is important to include the whole range of different forms of web archiving, and thereby also to show that not only automated approaches, but also traditional historical approaches to the archived web are still very useful. What is needed is for historians in general to become familiar with the distinctive features of the archived web, and for a rethinking of the traditional historiographic skills and methods to take the archived web into consideration.

Once the foregoing is established, historians may start to integrate the history web and web history—that is, to focus on how the online web can support historical studies of all sorts of digital sources, including the web itself. Such a "history web history" would need an online, web-based toolbox where the digitized, born-digital, and reborn digital may be seamlessly combined, with a view to facilitating cross-collection analysis and dissemination.

2   The Digital and the Web

To understand the archived web's specific characteristics as a digital medium, and how it may be used as a historical source, it is important to begin by considering how the digital, as such, may be understood. Based on a theoretical approach that understands the digital 0/1 as the two characters of an alphabet, it is argued that each type of digital medium is a digital medium in a specific way—each has its digitality—and that this digitality sets up the array of possible ways of interacting with the medium, including the researcher's interaction with the archived web. Therefore, when setting out to investigate the possible use of the archived web as a historical source, it is crucial to identify the archived web's digitality. A first step toward this is to introduce the concept of digitality, which I do in this chapter, where digitality is also used as a stepping-stone to conceptualizing a broader landscape of digital media with three clusters of digital media types—digitized, born-digital, and reborn digital media.[1] And since the archived web originates from the online web, it is important to identify the characteristics of the online web, which I do toward the end of this chapter.

2.1   Digitality

It is striking how much has been published in recent years about new cultural objects such as "digital media" and about new academic fields such as "digital humanities"—or more generally, about "digital" and "X"—but how little effort has been put into reflecting on the core of these novelties, the digital itself. Paradoxically, understanding "digital" seems to have fallen by the wayside.

From a mechanical point of view, the digital in modern computers originates from the specific way electricity is used in the digital artifact.

Electricity-based media have existed for over a century, from the electric telegraph and the landline telephone, to radio and television, but these media have used electricity to make the machinery "run," such as the telegraph's perforation of a paper tape, or the changing illumination of dots on a television screen. This is also partly the case with the digital computer— for instance, with regard to the mouse, the keyboard, and the screen—but electricity is also used as a distinct unit in the central power circuit of the computer: either there is power or no power between two points.[2] This absence/presence of power is usually transcribed as the two discrete entities 0 and 1 that constitute the two binary digits—bits—that are the point of departure for developing digital artifacts.[3]

According to Finnemann, the binary notation 0/1 is part of an informational rather than a formal notation system, the difference being that the units of a formal notation system, such as the binary number system, carry values in themselves (0=0, 1=1), whereas this is not the case in an informal notation system:

> While a formal notation unit is defined as a physical representation of a semantic value, informational units are defined as physical forms which are legitimate units but without any semantic value of their own. On the other hand, they need to be defined as mechanical operative units in the physical machine. (Finnemann, 1999, p. 144)

In this sense, the binary notation 0/1 may be considered the two characters of an alphabet. Since letters are characterized by being devoid of meaning as such, they lack any semantic content of their own, but when combined in sequences of words, sentences, and texts, meaning is created (cf. Finnemann 1999, pp. 144–148).[4] Since modern computers operate by using power as a distinct unit, the characters 0/1 are physical operative units, and therefore, on a very fundamental level, computers literally write and read with power. Additionally, and in contrast to a linguistic alphabet, the characters 0/1 may be used to represent any form of semantic expression, such as images and sounds, and not just written texts (Finnemann, 1999, p. 145). In this sense, digital images are (also) texts (Finnemann, 1999, pp. 149–152). This particular use of electricity as a writing/reading device in modern computers is what makes digital media distinct from nondigital media, including electronic media.

All digital media artifacts, including the web, share the characters 0/1, but as with print media, where all books and texts are not identical just because they share the same letters of an alphabet, all digital artifacts are not identical just because they share the characters 0/1. Therefore, it is not enough to characterize digital media by insisting that they share the 0 and 1. Instead, an analysis of digital media must, on the one hand, acknowledge this fundamental level of digital writing/reading and include it where relevant, but, on the other hand, it must investigate how these shared fundamental building blocks materialize in a media artifact and are combined and processed as a text in each specific case. In the present context, the term *digitality* is used to capture the specific ways in which the digital bits are materialized and combined in a concrete media artifact and in concrete texts.[5]

2.1.1   The Double Duality of Digitality

To extend the foregoing line of theoretical thought, the digitality of digital media may be characterized by two types of duality, one that relates to their material nature as *media* artifacts, and one that revolves around the nature and the layers of *text* they can convey. Knowledge of both aspects of digitality is important, since each in its way establishes a framework for how users may interact with the digital medium and the digital text.[6]

The first type of digital media duality is that of digital media being simultaneously material artifacts and digital. Although the digital writing of 0 and 1 is never experienced by humans in its pure form, as power/no power, it is there and it is indispensable. What is experienced is the artifact, the machine. On the web, and in any other digital media type, the digital is always already embedded in a material artifact, made of glass, plastic, metal, or the like, combined to form mainframe computers, laptops, CD-ROMs, cables, wireless networks, smartphones, and similar.

The first type of digital media duality is concerned with the digital and its materializations in different layers of materiality, from the home of the digital that facilitates the functioning of the physical operational digital alphabet—large circuitboards with a maze of plugged-in cables, or integrated circuits—to the outer material characteristics of the artifact, such as a metal box with a certain size and weight, and a host of input/output devices, each of which has an impact on the possible use of the digital medium—for instance, its mobility, how easy or time consuming its use is, or how easy it is to manipulate.[7] Thus, although digital media are digital, they are also always nondigital.

The second type of digital media duality is that of digital texts (in digital media). A digital text is always something that may be experienced and interacted with by a reader, listener, or user through various output devices such as screen, speakers, or mouse, somewhat similar to nondigital media texts. But it is also composed of various layers of digital text "underneath" the experienced text, from the binary text written with 0s and 1s to various layers of software code and text treated by the software, which is eventually translated into the visible/audible text. In contrast to nondigital mechanical media that have only one layer of text, such as the writing and images we see on a book page or a television screen, digital media have extra layers of text, namely, the hidden digital texts below the text experienced by the reader.[8]

Two important points should be noted. First, the binary text is not readable (or is hardly readable) by humans, but it is machine-readable. As we move up through the layers of software code and data, texts become increasingly human- and machine-readable at the same time, although not readable to the end user but only to specialists who are able to read programming languages, until these texts eventually end up being human-understandable semantic and formal units on our computer screens in the form of images, graphics, and written words. Second, and in continuation of the above, the text experienced by humans is always presented at the expense of the various layers of machine- and human-readable digital texts, which are pushed into the background in order to foreground the experienced text. Thus, computer end users have no immediate experience of all the underlying layers, although they provide the indispensable condition of what can be experienced.

In summary, all digital media share the foregoing two types of duality, and the ways a given digital medium combines the digital alphabet in material and textual forms define the medium's digitality.[9]

As a consequence of these two types of duality, a study of digital media may focus on the first or second duality alone, or on their interplay. Taking the first case, that could include studies of the interaction between the nondigital and digital sides of digital media artifacts, like the materiality of the hard drive and the inscriptions and erasures it allows for, as discussed in Matthew Kirschenbaum's *Mechanisms: New Media and the Forensic Imagination* (2008). Other examples might include the digital hard drive viewed in a longer historical perspective, with a focus on the material devices that preceded it (Allen-Robertson, 2017), or the web archeology project to restore "De Digitale Stad," the digital city of Amsterdam, by using original servers, hard drives, and tapes (cf. de Haan, 2016; Alberts et al., 2017). The second case could include studies of software and the various semiotic expressions generated when software is executed, such as text documents, images, web pages, and interactive applications (e.g., Manovich, 2013). Or one may choose to study the interplay between the media material and the textual side of digital media, such as how the size of smartphone screens affects displayed content and its perception (e.g., Naylor & Sanchez, 2017), or how the QWERTY keyboard (and the associated ASCII characters) delayed the spread of the internet in countries with "Han"-character-based scripts, such as China and Japan (McLelland, 2017).

An exhaustive analysis of a given digital medium's digitality will include, first, the material artifact itself, and its ways of enabling the use of the digital alphabet, second, the signifying systems of the experienced text and the hidden textual layers that enable it, and third, the mutual and continuous interaction and interdependence of these two dualities.

In this book's analysis of the archived web's digitality, I focus primarily on the duality related to the text, mainly because what goes into a web archive is the web as text, and not the material artifacts that locate and distribute the web (mainframe computers, routers, cables, etc.). However, the latter are included where relevant.

2.1.2 Forms of Digitality: Digitized, Born-Digital, Reborn Digital

The concept of digitality means that not all digital media are digital in the same way, just because they are digital. But despite their differences, digital media also share a number of similarities that make it possible to group them. Since this book is concerned with how different digital sources became digital, I use a typology based on the provenance of the different types of digital texts. I distinguish among three types—digitized, born-digital, and reborn digital material—each of which may be subdivided.

Digitized material is material that previously existed in a nondigital form, but has been transformed to become digital. For instance, the nondigital original may be handwritten documents, print media, or analog electronic audiovisual media such as radio and television, and they may have been digitized in a number of ways, from being entered with a keyboard and transferred to punch cards, to the scanning of documents, prints, and photographs to create image files, or the digital recording of analog sound and moving images. Artifacts may have been digitized to become ordinary or 3D pictures. It is not unusual for an original to still exist, which may be referenced as a baseline, in cases of doubt about the quality of the digitization (for reflections on digitized collections, see Hockey, 2000, pp. 11–23; Terras, 2012). The main characteristic of digitized material is that, to a large extent, its digitality is a function of the nature of the original. Although all digitized material has a nondigital provenance, there are differences in terms of textuality as a function of the nondigital original. For instance, although both a scanned newspaper and a recorded radio program may be preserved as individual files, the way the machine-readable files are interpreted and read when made human-readable and the way they are presented at the interface level will be different, because newspapers and radio programs are fundamentally different before being digitized, and these differences do not disappear because they now share the digital alphabet. Once digitized, additional layers of text may be added, such as various markups or optical character recognition (OCR), where light and dark areas of an image file are identified as characters and converted to letters of ASCII code. But it is important to bear in mind that these are added to something already digitized; they are not part of the nondigital original (see also section 2.2).

Born-digital material is material that has never existed in any form other than digital. Born-digital material was created for and made available on digital media only, such as CD-ROMs, DVDs, or computer networks.[10] Therefore, this type of material does not have any nondigital original to refer to. The digitality of born-digital media varies, from computer games on DVDs, to the web or apps on smartphones, and there are subtypes. For instance, on the web there are differences between Facebook, Twitter, and a website (the textuality of the web as born-digital material is further elaborated in the following section).

Reborn digital material is born-digital material that has been collected and preserved, and that has been changed in this process to such an extent that it is not identical to the born-digital material from which it was made. This could be an emulated computer game, a screen filming of an app, or material in a web archive. A born-digital original may exist for this type of digital medium, but in many cases this original is ephemeral; it may have been changed or even have disappeared after its collection and preservation. To a large extent, the digitality of this type of material is a function of the nexus between the digitality of the born-digital material from which it was made and the process of transformation, hence its reborn character.

Distinguishing among the three specific types of digital material is important, because the digitality of each type has a decisive impact on how they may be interacted with when they are being collected and preserved and made available, for instance to researchers who want to use them as historical sources. Digitizing a collection of newspapers, filming an app on a smartphone, and archiving an online website are three different things, and thus the results of the three processes will have to be approached differently when analyzed, including which digital tools can be used, since their possible application is a function of the material's specific digitality.[11]

2.2   Digitality of the Web

To fully understand the digitality of the web in its archived form, the reborn web, it is imperative to understand the digitality of the online web in its born-digital form. The reason for this is that since the reborn web is a transformation of the born-digital web, the digitality of the latter constitutes the condition for the digitality of the archived web, in combination with the archiving process itself (see chapter 5).

One way of characterizing the web is by focusing on the three technical components on which it is based: the hypertext transfer protocol (HTTP), the uniform resource locator/identifier (URL/URI), and the hypertext markup language (HTML). Despite their developments over time, the various historical instances of these three constitute the technological system that enables the transfer of files from one computer to another by the use of an addressing system, as well as the "translation" of these files into something that may be viewed in a web browser.[12]

Taking the nexus between the web understood in technical terms and the web as experienced by a user as the points of departure, the digitality of the online web is characterized by three distinctive features that are closely knit together: the web has two textual layers, it is fragmented, and it is hyperlinked.

2.2.1   The Web Is Born with Two Textual Layers

The layered nature of all digital texts based on the transformation from bits into more extended code forms comes in a specific form with the online web. From the point of view of the user, the web consists of two layers of text: the text immediately visible in a browser window (or audible through speakers),[13] and the text that enables the visible text to appear in the browser, namely the text written in HTML, the document-layout and hyperlink-specification markup language of the web.[14]

When a web address is typed in the location bar of a web browser and the Enter key is pressed, the computer contacts the relevant web server and asks for a specific HTML file, and then this file and the associated files or similar (if any), such as graphics, streaming, feeds, or the like, are returned from the web server to the computer, where they are interpreted in the web browser and replayed as a web page, displaying letters, graphics, images, and so on, positioned at the right locations.[15]

One could argue that strictly speaking, the web has only one layer of text, the hidden text (HTML, the textual content between HTML tags, and associated files), but if the web is to be understood by a user—in the present instance, a researcher who wants to use it as a historical source—the visible text presented in the browser has to be included in an understanding of the online web's digitality. (As noted in section 2.1, the software code also has to be seen as executed software.)

A closer look at the two layers of text makes it evident that they are constituted as texts in two very different ways.

The text the user sees on the screen (or hears through speakers) may include any form of expression, including letters and words, still images, moving images, and sound, and a variety of forms of interaction, such as clicking and scrolling. Additionally, the semiotic elements do not have to follow a predetermined order; they may be placed haphazardly on the web page. In contrast, text written in HTML may be made up of only written letters and symbols, to compose words and tags such as <p></p> or <a></a> that begin and end a paragraph or a hyperlink, respectively, and it has to follow a predetermined sequence and comply with certain rules. Although the digital text seen in the browser is not machine-readable as such, the HTML text is by default machine-readable and readable by humans, although the latter only if the reader has knowledge of this specific programming language.

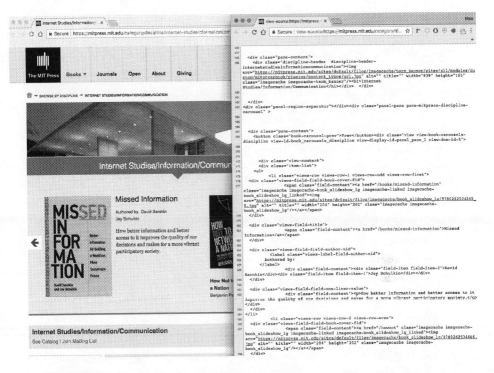

Figure 2.1
An MIT Press web page with its underlying source code.

In addition to the foregoing, the following should be noted. First, the HTML text disappears when interpreted in a web browser to enable the visible text to be displayed, but it may still be viewed in most modern web browsers, either by selecting "View source code" or similar, or by opening the HTML file in an HTML editor. Second, although the HTML code may be readable, it may be difficult for an inexperienced reader to see exactly how the HTML is translated when interpreted by a browser. Third, the relationship between the entire HTML code and what is displayed in the browser is not 1:1, since not every element of the code is shown directly in the browser. In some cases, code may be made visible—for example, by mousing over it—or it may remain hidden from the web user but still be active and influence what is appearing in the browser window. This means that from an analytical point of view, a web page's information that is not immediately visible on screen constitutes a kind of built-in markup, a sort of metadata, but less systematic than the usual metadata, such as The Dublin

Core Metadata Initiative. Thus, to a certain extent, the web comes with its own metadata (after all, HTML is a markup language). Finally, it should be noted that HTML is not the only digital layer that allows a web page to be transferred from one computer to another, since HTML sits on top of other digital layers related to transmission, such as network, transport, and session layers, just as each of the many objects of which a web page may be composed, such as image and sound files, comes with a layer of digital text. But HTML is specific to the web, even if it relies on and includes other digital layers.

The two layers of web text are among the places where the web is distinct from digitized material. Both digitized material and the online web include visible (or audible) text, but what happens "beneath" this text differs. In the case of a scanned document such as a newspaper, the scanning captures an image and converts it into an image file, usually in the form of a bitmap, and this bitmap is what is read by the display software that shows the scanned newspaper. In contrast, the web comes with an extra layer of text between the bits and what is presented in the web browser, namely the textual layer of a markup language, the HTML. Thus, on the machine-readable levels of text, the digitized texts tend to be "flatter," since they basically consist of a bitmap, whereas the online web is born with a programming layer on top of the bits—a markup language that is human- and machine-readable.

Extra layers may be added to a digitized file, such as an OCR layer on a pdf file, which is also an extra hidden digital layer "on top" of the visible text, but there are two major differences from the web: it is not an indispensable and inherent part of the original document but is added after digitization, and it is much less rich in terms of the information it holds (about OCR, see Cordell, 2017). Thus, the two layers of the web text create opportunities for an analysis of the textuality of the web, where the digital text may be "read" in three ways: the visible text presented in the browser window(s) can be read, the HTML text may be investigated as such, and the relation between the two may be examined (i.e., how certain parts of the HTML code or a file condition and render the manifest text).

2.2.2   The Web Is Born Fragmented
A distinctive feature of the web is its fragmented nature. From the point of view of the user, what is presented in a web browser may appear as a

collection of various semiotic fragments—a heading, an image, graphics—
that may (or may not) create a coherent semiotic unit. However, the fact
that on the visible level a web page is composed of smaller individual elements is not specific to the web, but may be found in other media types,
like a printed newspaper page. In a web browser, though, what appears
to be a unified page with various semiotic elements is not only produced
by a hidden text of a very different nature, as mentioned above. It is also
patched together by the textual elements in the HTML file and by a number
of bits and pieces that may be retrieved from the same web server or from
other web servers, such as graphics, written text, image or video files, feeds,
and streamed audiovisual material. Thus, beneath the visible assemblage of
semiotic elements, the web page is constituted as a much more fundamental collection of fragments.

On the one hand, the fragmented nature of the web is systematically
inscribed in the HTML file in the form of machine-readable tags, which
means that whatever is placed between tags constitutes a textual fragment,
like a hyperlink reference (<a>), the title of the HTML document (<title>),
or a video (<video>). Thus, the core file type of the online web, the HTML
file, comes with nicely cut and separate fragments, each of which may
cause an element to be shown in the visible text, and each of which may
be studied separately. On the other hand, the variety of files attached to the
HTML file (by linking) also adds to the fragmentation. Since the HTML text
itself cannot contain expressions other than written text (see above), other
types of expressions, such as images, video, and sound, must be retrieved as
individual files, streams, or feeds, based on a command in the HTML code,
and must be displayed in the right place. It is worth noting that each of
these files, streams, and feeds embedded in a web page comes with its own
web address, which is different from that of the HTML file, which is why
they constitute individual fragments in their own right, as clearly identifiable units outside the HTML code. And they usually also contain other sorts
of information that may be relevant when studying the web, such as file
names or file type extensions that may help identify the file type.[16]

As is now evident, what may appear to be fragments on the manifest
textual level in a web browser window are fragmented in a much more fundamental sense below this visible text. Everything presented on the visible
web page is mirrored as a fragment in the HTML code, but as the HTML
code as such recedes into the background when a web page is shown in the

browser, the fragmented state of the web page is not experienced because the bits and pieces are seamlessly stitched together.

Finally, two things have to be observed about these two forms of fragmentation. First, the array of possible fragments is heterogeneous, since it may consist of all tags in the HTML code and a great number of file types. Second, fragmentation may work on every part of the displayed web page, and therefore there is not necessarily a 1:1 relation between what constitutes a fragment on the visible and the hidden levels. One semiotic element on the visible level, such as a photograph, need not correlate with one file, since a photograph may be composed of several image files, just as segments of a photograph may be tagged, whereby a segment of the photograph constitutes a fragment in its own right.[17]

The fragmented nature of the web is also distinct from digitized materials. In contrast to digitized collections, where fragmentation is not an inherent part of the material but may be added after digitization, for instance as markup, the online web is born in a fragmentary state on various levels. On a scanned newspaper page it may be difficult to separate images, headings, and graphics from the body text, because such a separation was not an inherent part of the original paper version, and in any case it has to be done after digitization, whereas in many ways this is an easier task with the online web (and later with the archived web as well). However, a major difference is that the fragmenting of a digitized collection may be done in a systematic and controlled way, whereas on the web, things are messier in this respect.

2.2.3   The Web Is Born Hyperlinked

The third inherent feature of the web is the hyperlink—that is, the ability to connect two fragments on the same or on different computers. For millennia, references between textual units have existed in various media forms, but what is specific to the web hyperlink is that when using an HTML code to connect link source to link target, two textual entities are connected in a very concrete and direct manner. The hyperlink is just one fragment among other web fragments, but it is a very important one, since it is the thread of which the web is woven.[18]

It may be argued that the hyperlink is not a necessity for the functioning of the web, and thus not an inherent part of the web. Although it is true that one could navigate the web without the use of hyperlinks, it would be a very cumbersome task, because the exact web address would have to be entered in the location bar every time one wanted to go to another web location, and a page with search results would be very difficult to handle for the same reason. Thus the hyperlink is de facto an inherent part of the web.

It should be noted that the hyperlink is present on the two textual layers in different ways. On the visible layer, the hyperlink may be immediately visible and signal that it is the first step in a connection by the use of underlining, boldface, a specific color, a specific frame around a picture, or a similar device. Or it may be visible only under certain circumstances, such as when the presence of a hyperlink is only evident when moused over and the cursor changes to a hand with a pointing finger, or other pointing features. These ways of making the hyperlink source visible vary with the shifting conventions of web design and technical options.

The hyperlink need not be immediately visible on a web page as seen in a browser window, but it will always be clearly and unambiguously present in the invisible text as a piece of code. In the main, on the code level, hyperlinks come in two different forms. On the one hand, there are hyperlinks that can bring web content from another location to the user if the user deliberately and intentionally activates the hyperlink. This is the click-jump link (the <a> tag), where the user clicks on a link source and then jumps to the link target (although what actually happens is that the content from the link target is retrieved to the user's computer). On the other hand, hyperlinks may bring web content from elsewhere to the user's computer without any activity on the part of the user, and without indicating that this is actually what happens. This is the case with HTML commands that link to and automatically retrieve material from outside the HTML page (by the use of the <embed> tag). In this case, the result of this hidden hyperlinking may or may not be evident to the user. The first happens when retrieved images, streamed video/audio, or various forms of feeds are displayed; the latter occurs with any form of continuous linking, where the hyperlink establishes a communication session with another web server and sends information back and forth based on user behavior, such as cookies and a variety of tracker technologies.

As indicated above with regard to the fragmented nature of the web, any part of a web page may be fragmented, and this also affects hyperlinks. Hyperlinks inherit and support the fragmentation of the web, since the presence of the invisible code text enables hyperlinks to "graft" onto anything shown in the web browser, be it one letter in a sentence or any segment of a photograph, not just clearly delimited semiotic units such as words or images (see Brügger, 2017a, p. 22). One extra point deserves to be highlighted in relation to the web's hyperlinked nature: the hyperlink is not only the cornerstone of the online web, it is also an indispensable prerequisite for one of the most important forms of collecting and preserving the web, namely, web crawling, because web crawling is based on following hyperlinks (see section 5.3.2). Finally, as was the case with the two layers of the web and fragmentation, the presence of hyperlinks as an inherent element of the web makes it distinct from digitized material. In a digitized collection hyperlinks are a possible add-on—for instance, they may be added to a collection of scanned newspapers—but with the web they are an inherent element in such a way that if removed, the web would no longer be the web.

In summary, the web is born with three "relatively fixed features"—it comes with two layers of text, it is fragmented, and it is hyperlinked—and the three features are interconnected and interdependent in various ways. For example, the retrieval of fragments is based on HTML code and hyperlinks, and the HTML code enables the patching of the visible web text. As will be shown in the following chapters, all three invariant traits of the online web's digitality have a bearing on how the web may be archived and later used as a historical source.

3   Five Analytical Web Strata

The web does not present itself as a phenomenon with clear and obvious demarcations indicating how a study of it should be focused. Unlike written documents, print media, or radio/television, where analytical objects such as "page," "image," "article," and "program" seem the obvious focal points, the web does not lend itself to such straightforward and taken-for-granted ways of approaching it analytically. Therefore, what researchers who want to study the web need is a set of theoretical, systematic subdivisions in manageable and coherent units that may help to focus web studies, and that goes for both the online web and the archived web.

From a technological point of view, the web may be considered a collection of billions of files sitting on a very large number of web servers from which they are requested and retrieved to the users' computers. However, understanding the web as merely a collection of files does not say much about the web as presented in a browser for a user, including a researcher.

This chapter proposes an analytical grid with five analytical web strata, which takes the web as a textual phenomenon as its point of departure. And since the web comes with two distinct textual layers—the visible/audible web in the browser, and the hidden text of the HTML code and associated files—so do the five web strata. Thus, what is termed "web element," "web page," "website," "web sphere," and the "web as a whole" may be identified as both the visible web in the browser (figure 3.1) and the hidden text that enables the visible web (figure 3.2).

It should be emphasized that the above-mentioned stratification of the web is concerned only with how the researcher may delimit the web as an object of study. How this object is then analyzed in detail depends on the investigator's research questions and on the theories and methods that are

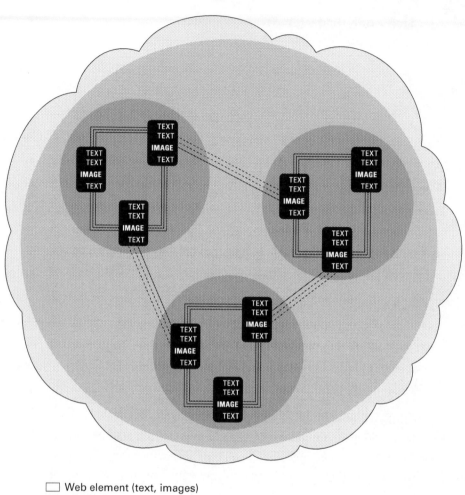

☐ Web element (text, images)
■ Web page
▨ Website
▨ Web sphere
▨ Web as a whole

Figure 3.1
The five visible analytical web strata

applied to understand this object. Concrete examples of web history studies of each of the five strata are presented in chapter 4.

Figure 3.1 shows the five visible web strata: web element, web page, website, web sphere, and the web as a whole. The lines connecting the website's web pages indicate the semantic, formal, and physical performative interrelations, whereas the three lines between the web sphere's websites indicate the semantic as well as the possible formal and physical performative interrelations in the web sphere (the latter two lines are dotted to indicate that these relations are only possible).

3.1   The Visible Web Strata

The web element is the first of the five web strata identifiable by the researcher in the heterogeneous raw material that constitutes the visible web. An individual web element may be any coherent semiotic entity in the form of a written element, a static image element, a moving image element, or a sound element. Thus, web elements may include a heading, menu items, a written body text (the entire text, a paragraph, a sentence), an image, a piece of graphics, a banner ad, or a video. How the individual web element may be delimited as such—that is, as a coherent semiotic entity—depends on a combination of semantic, formal, and physical performative features. These features can include the use of textual cohesion or grammatical and lexical coherence (semantics); typography, line breaks, lines, or image frames (formal); or various kinds of continuous movements or discontinuous "jumps," such as scrolling or clicking/hyperlinks/mouseovers (physically performative).[1] A study of web elements may focus either on understanding the characteristics of the individual web elements as such or on how elements relate to each other.[2]

The web element is positioned on a web page, the second web stratum. A web page is whatever is presented within the frame of a single browser window. Thus, the individual web page is delimited in a very formal way by the borders of the individual browser window, and not by any semantic means related to whatever is actually presented in the window. Although the word *page* is used, this does not imply that "web page" is only understood as a page in a handwritten document or print medium. Since moving images in the form of ads, games, or video may also be presented in a browser window, "web page" is understood in a very broad sense, including all types of web elements that a web browser can display in a window. A study of a web page may focus on the web elements presented within the browser window—for instance, the use of specific types or forms of elements (mainly text, images, video), or the overall combination of elements in what one might term the overall composition of the web page.

The third web stratum is the website, which is an analytical unit composed of interrelated web pages. The interrelations that keep the individual web pages together to form a website are underpinned along the same three lines as mentioned above in relation to the web element. That is, the web pages are connected by semantic, formal, and physically performative means, and the more consistent these three types of interrelations are, the more clearly the website is delimited (see Brügger, 2009, p. 122). Thus, what delimits the website as such is the extent to which a number of web pages treat the same subject (semantic cohesion), resemble each other (formal cohesion), and make it possible to go from one web page to another (physically performative cohesion). A study of a website may focus on what characterizes the web pages (all/a selection), and on each or all three forms of interrelations.

If one studies the fourth stratum, the web sphere, the focus is on the web material—web elements, web pages, or websites—related to a topic, a theme, an event, or a geographic area, such as a political election, a sports event, catastrophes, or a city, region, or nation. This understanding of the web sphere is inspired by Kirsten Foot and Steven Schneider, who coined the term in 2006:

We conceptualize a web sphere as not simply a collection of websites, but as a set of dynamically defined digital resources spanning multiple websites deemed relevant or related to a central event, concept, or theme. Although some of these resources may be hyperlinked to each other ... links do not define the sphere. Rather, the boundaries of a web sphere are generally delimited by a shared topical orientation across web resources and a temporal framework. (Foot & Schneider, 2006, p. 20)

In the present context the "digital resources spanning multiple websites" are more specifically understood as web elements, web pages, and websites, as defined above. And the fact that these elements need not be hyperlinked to be part of the web sphere is rephrased here by maintaining that the elements of the web sphere need to be semantically interrelated ("a shared topical orientation"), though they may be interrelated by physically performative means ("links do not define the sphere"). The elements of the web sphere may also—at least in some cases and to some degree—share formal traits, as when an event, such as a sports event, or similar, has a logo that is used across websites (Foot and Schneider do not include this in their definition). Also, as indicated in the quote above, Foot and Schneider conceptualize the event, concept, or theme as delimited by time ("a temporal framework"), but in the present context the web sphere need not be (but may be) delimited by time. However, as specified above, the web sphere may also be delimited by geographic space, such as a city, region, nation, or other geographic entity; although geography may be included in the broad categories "concept or theme," it is worth spelling it out as a specific way of delimiting the web sphere. Thus, the web sphere is delimited by a shared event, concept, theme, or geographic area, and it may be underpinned by formal forms of expressions and by hyperlinks connecting the elements. A study of a web sphere may focus on all strata in themselves, and on the ways they are interrelated to form the web sphere.

Finally, web studies may focus on the fifth web stratum, the web as a whole—that is, phenomena that transcend the other strata, such as the textual content seen in a web browser, the web browser itself, search algorithms, or even the web's total content. In contrast to the web element, website, and web sphere, the web as a whole is not delimited by any kind of consistent semantic, formal, or physically performative interrelations.

3.2 The Hidden Web Strata

On the hidden textual level of the web, the first of the web strata—the web element—is constituted by the previously mentioned fragments (section 2.2), namely, HTML text and other individual files. The hidden web element takes three forms. First, it may be any delimited element of code, for instance, defined by tags, such as a hyperlink (<a>) or a video (<video>); second, it may be any piece of written content, either content also shown in the browser when the element is rendered (body text, headings, page title) or invisible content, such as keywords or descriptions in metatags; third, the web element may consist of any type of file associated with the HTML file, such as text, image, graphic, PowerPoint, sound, video files, or other. These web elements are clearly delimited either by HTML tags or by file extensions. A study of the hidden web elements may focus on each of the above—for example, it could be a study of hyperlinks, of the content of headings, or of the number of image files.

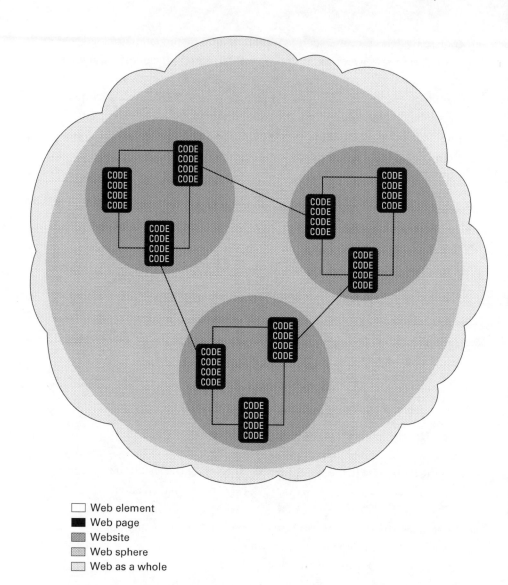

Web element
Web page
Website
Web sphere
Web as a whole

Figure 3.2
The five hidden analytical web strata

Figure 3.2 shows the five hidden web strata. The lines between the website's web pages and between the web sphere's websites indicate that the interrelations between these entities must be expressed on the code level.

The second web stratum, that of the web page, consists of the code for the entire page as such, as expressed by an individual HTML file. This file could include a style sheet that describes the presentation of the web page, such as a cascading style sheet (CSS), or frames, which were much in use in the late 1990s, or information about the size of the browser window (length/width) or about background color or image. The hidden level of the web page is delimited by the HTML file, and one may decide to study the composition of the web page on a code level.

On the hidden level, the third web stratum—the website—is constituted by whatever code element supports the coherence of the web pages across the website, such as the web domain name, a general template, a content management system (CMS), blog software, and the like. On the code level, the coherence of the website is supported mainly by these features, in combination with actually expressed hyperlinks to other web pages on the website, and thus the website is delimited by these means.

The web sphere, the fourth web stratum, must be constituted by something that may be used to delimit the event, concept, theme, or geographic area on the code level. This may include any type of body text, a set of URLs, a top-level domain name (e.g., a country-code top-level domain (ccTLD) such as .uk, .fr, .dk, or a generic top-level domain (gTLD) such as .com, .gov), a subdomain name (e.g., .gov.uk, .ac.uk), or the web sphere may be created by the use of outgoing hyperlinks to find relevant members to include in the web sphere. Thus, a code-level study of the web sphere may involve all the above components, only one, or combinations.

Finally, the fifth web stratum, the web as a whole, comprises hidden-level phenomena that transcend the other strata—for instance, the web protocols and standards that run the web servers and the communication between them, the rules of the HTML programming language, and the use of programming languages other than HTML, such as JavaScript.

3.3   Visible/Hidden Web Strata

The five web strata of the two distinct textual levels share a number of similarities, yet they also have differences. First, it should be emphasized that on both the visible and the hidden levels, the strata are interwoven, as each stratum constitutes the context for the other strata: the web page is the background for web elements, the website is composed of web pages with web elements, and the web sphere may be made up of web elements, web pages, and websites. One may wish to study each stratum as such—for instance, images or specific file types—or one could decide to focus on several strata at the same time, either giving them equal weight, or with one or more as the main focus. For example, a study of 50 mainstream newspaper websites might focus on how images (web element) relate to the web page on which they are positioned (web page), how they are interlinked to other web elements and pages on the newspaper's website (website), and how this relates to similar websites (web sphere). Or, on the hidden level, this might include image files, the HTML files of individual web pages, the relevant information related to the website, and a web sphere delimited by some of the parameters mentioned above.

Second, on both visible and hidden textual levels, the web strata are essentially concerned with how the web may be defined as different analytical objects, and not with how the "content" of each of the strata is actually generated. For example, when it is maintained that the web page is whatever is presented in a browser window (visible) or is constituted by an HTML file (hidden), this indicates only the focus of the study, and not how the web elements became part of a given web page, be it because they were part of a "flat" HTML page, or because they were being pulled in from other web servers, based on a piece of HTML code. Thus, to identify the web page as an analytical unit does not itself imply that it is considered either a "static" or "dynamic" web page, but it helps retain a systematic analytical focus on the web page as such. The researcher can then decide to analyze the web page in its "static" form as it was shown in a browser, or in its "dynamic" form—that is, how it is constantly being reshaped and is in a state of flux because of being continuously in contact with a wider web environment in the form of other web servers that supply specific web elements.

Third, it should be emphasized that web strata, visible as well as hidden, are not about the amount of web material being studied, but about the focus of the study, since the amount of data cuts across the strata. For instance, one may focus a study on one small web element, such as images on web pages, but then decide to study the use of images on either 10 or 10,000 web pages.

To extend the last point made, one of the major differences between the strata on the two textual layers becomes clear, namely that for the most part, focusing on the visible strata does not scale. If one wants to study the use of images on 10 web pages, this is doable on the visible level, but if the study includes the use of images on 10,000 web pages, looking closely at each web image is not an option. Thus, when scaling up to amounts of web material that exceed what is possible to examine manually, in general only the hidden level is studied, mainly because it is already machine-readable and may be processed automatically.[3] This difference in scale resembles the distinction between close and distant reading introduced by literary scholar Franco Moretti (2000), but in the case of the web, a close reading may focus on either the visible or the hidden textual layer, or both, for instance to check the code that generates a specific web element, but as one moves toward a distant reading, only the hidden layer may be used.[4] However, with regard to this point, it is worth noting that an exclusive focus on either of the two layers comes at a price, namely the neglect of the other layer. Therefore, the most extended analyses will include both layers, but as mentioned, typically this is possible only at a small scale, since large amounts of web data may be approached only on the code level, which comes at the expense of losing the visible side of things. For instance, in an analysis of a large hyperlink network based on studying hyperlinks at the code level, the visible side of the nodes that are interlinked tends to disappear (see the examples in section 4.4).

The imbalance between the two textual levels with regard to scale leads to the identification of another difference. When studying only the visible web in a web browser, this object of study may be approached with the methods usually used to study visual artifacts, from intuitive and impressionistic approaches to a systematic content analysis. However, in cases where the code must be included to answer a research question related to one of the visible strata, this research question has to be translated into an equivalent on the code level. What is at stake here is a question of operationalizing the web's two layers—that is, of how to go from one layer to the other. For instance, a research project with a research question related to a clearly delimited web element on the visible level, say images, must find a way to operationalize this web element on the hidden level. In some cases this may be easily done, in particular if a clearly delimited counterpart exists on the hidden level, such as a specific tag, but this is not always true, as when the natural language in the body text is studied. And the reverse is also the case—that is, if a research project is guided by a research question related to something that is a clearly delimited web element on the code level, say a JavaScript, the question is how this actually translates to what happens on the visible layer. Thus, the challenge for the researcher is to translate from one layer to another by operationalizing a research question either as code or as a visible element.

Finally, two additional differences between the strata on the two textual layers must be mentioned. First, since the visible textual layer is directed toward the user, the delimitations and the coherence of each of the web strata are by and large a human-only matter, based on how the user understands the semantic, the formal, and the physical performative features of what is seen in a web browser. In contrast, these delimitations related to the human experience do not play any role on the hidden level, which is why the hidden web strata have to be expressed in a machine-readable way. Second, on the code level the web strata tend to be richer than is actually displayed on the visual level, simply because the code of, say, a web page, may contain a large number of web elements that are not necessarily shown in the web browser, but that may nevertheless be objects of study in their own right, such as metatags, a language code, or a tracking code. Thus, as mentioned above (section 2.2), there is no 1:1 relation between the two layers.

In summary, for a researcher who wants to study the web in its online and archived forms, it is possible to focus on all five web strata, either exclusively in their visual or hidden form, or in their various interrelated forms.

4   Cases of Web History

Before characterizing in greater detail the digitality of the archived web and how it impacts its scholarly use as a source, it is time to provide an overview of some typical examples of web history studies. Therefore, this chapter presents a variety of cases of web history, in both senses of the term. The cases are seen through the lens of this book's theoretical framework, as outlined in the previous two chapters, and in addition to providing typical examples that illustrate the range of historical studies performed with the archived web as a source, they will be used to fuel the discussion of the archived web's digitality in the following chapters. Thus, what follows does not constitute a systematic or chronological review of the web history literature; instead each case in its own way illustrates how fundamental web historiography topics have been addressed in selected web history studies. The examples may serve as inspiration for historians who consider using the archived web in their studies.[1]

The presentation of the cases is structured according to the five web strata, and within each of the strata it is guided by whether the given study focuses on the visible or the hidden side of the web stratum in question (or both), and whether it is a case of web history as history with the web, or history of the web. It should also be noted that it is not always easy to determine which of the strata a given study focuses on. For instance, in some cases other strata are included indirectly or accidentally, with no explicit acknowledgment, such as when the web page is part of an analysis of web elements but receives no significant mention. In cases where it is clear that several strata are studied, they are introduced in the subsection on "Multiple-Strata Cases" (section 4.6).

Since writing history with the web is still in its infancy, there are only a limited number of cases to choose from, mainly because historians have to become familiar with the archived web and with how it may be used along-side other better-known source types. As Webster points out,

Historians using web archives are themselves in the process of understanding the nature of the material with which they must deal, and consequently have been less concerned with its integration with other kinds of sources. ... Use of the historic Web which is both diachronic and multi-modal must be the aim; only at that point will the enterprise look like historical research as commonly understood. (Webster, 2018, n.p.)

Finally, as mentioned above, this presentation of examples of web history looks only at cases where the archived web is a source, but it should be emphasized that there are a number of histories of the web based on a great variety of sources other than the archived web. Examples include histories of a web element (Brügger, 2017a), a website (Thorsen, 2010; Burns & Brügger, 2012; Deken, 2017), and the web as a whole (Natale & Bory, 2017; Barry, 2017; Halavais, 2018).

Toward the end of this chapter some of the trends in web history research are summarized, to provide a bridge to the web historiography topics discussed in the following chapters.

4.1   The Web Element

All four examples of historical studies of web elements presented below are histories of the web, and in each case the focus is on the visible (or audible) side of the archived web, although in different ways. Each example in its own way highlights important aspects of the use of the archived web as a historical source.

4.1.1   Banner Ads—Collecting the Web Yourself

In an article titled "Cultural Values in Internet Advertising: A Longitudinal Study of the Banner Ads of the Top U.S. Web Sites" (Li & Zhunag, 2007), Xigen Li and Lin Zhunag investigate the dominant cultural values of advertising on the web. The study maps the evolution of the use of banner ads on the top American websites in 2000, 2003, and 2007. The aim is not only to say something about banner ads as such, but also to understand these ads as they relate to general cultural trends and typical cultural norms of American society concerning advertising and the internet.

A unit of analysis is clearly defined—"one banner ad on the homepage of each web site" (Li & Zhunag, 2007, p. 64)—and the study is based on the archived web, but not as the web of the past appeared in an already established web collection. On the contrary, the researchers "collected" or "downloaded" the source material themselves while it was still online (Li & Zhunag, 2007, p. 63): 302 ads in 2000, 262 in 2003, and 302 in 2007, in all cases based on a random sample. However, how the collection and downloads were done is not specified—for instance, what software was used, and in which form the collected banner ads were preserved. Questions related to the rapid change of this particular web element are also addressed:

Banner ads on web sites "decay" or are updated very quickly. ... Through an observation of the 10 web sites out of the top 100 one month before data collection, we found that in five minutes, the numbers of unduplicated banner ads appeared on the home page of a web site ranged from zero to 12. (Li & Zhunag, 2007, p. 63)

Therefore, the archiving interval was set to five minutes for each website.

Li and Zhunag's study clearly illustrates how web history took place in the years right after the turn of the millennium. Researchers often had to establish their own collection of the web of the past before it actually became the web of the past, mainly because the number of web archives was limited, and if collections existed they were often not detailed enough and researcher access was not widespread. Therefore, the authors do not reflect at all on whether a web archive could have been used, and with good reason, since the most obvious option for providing relevant material, the Internet Archive, did not establish the first iteration of its replay software, the Wayback Machine (see section 7.2), until 2001, and so in a longitudinal study including the year 2000, this would not be particularly useful. Also, banner ads are rarely archived in any systematic way in web archives, if they are archived at all.

The rapid pace of change on the web is clearly acknowledged in Li and Zhunag's study, possibly because the object of study, the banner ad, is among the most rapidly changing types of web elements, and they also specify their archiving strategy (sample form and collection intervals). But they provide neither reflections on archiving form—the material was just "collected" or "downloaded"—nor on how it was preserved and how complete it may be. Finally, no information is included on where the data set may be found.

4.1.2 Screen Filming of Banner Ads

Web advertising is also the topic of a book chapter titled "The Aesthetics of Web Advertising: Methodological Implications for the Study of Genre Development" by Iben Bredahl Jessen (2010). This study adopts a different focus on web advertising than cultural values, since its aim is to analyze web ads from a media aesthetics perspective, with a view to understanding how they relate to existing media and genre conventions with regard to attracting the user's attention. The study understands web ads as broader than banner ads, and it proposes a typology of web ads in general. The chapter clearly maps the possible sources from which web ads may be collected, including the websites where the ads are found, ad servers, agencies, private collections, and web archives (Jessen, 2010, p. 260). However, as the author notes,

Principally, a web archive could also be a useful source for that purpose, especially in order to collect material with the aim of studying genre development. However, for the time being, web archiving seems to suffer from technical problems in harvesting, e.g., dynamic content as java scripts. (Jessen, 2010, p. 260)

Thus, the material to be studied was collected by the researcher herself. But because of the "dynamic and transient character of the web medium" (Jessen, 2010, p. 261), preserving web ads is not easy. The author decided to make screen recordings of the appearance and location of the ads and of their link target, combined with screenshots, mainly because the focus of the study was on the aesthetics of web ads, including the movements inside each individual web ad (possibilities of interaction, animation, or moving pictures), not on how they were interlinked (Jessen, 2010, p. 263). The result was two collections, one from 2004 to 2005 (with 1,025 ads) and one from 2008 to 2009 (221 ads), and the typology was established based on this material (Jessen, 2010, pp. 271–274). Jessen also discusses the constructed nature of what she collected, including the possible role of cookies, and she emphasizes that a systematic procedure has to be adopted when navigating a website to preserve web ads.

Jessen's study is an example of how a specific web element may be collected and analyzed, and it illustrates the importance of accompanying the analysis with a high level of methodological reflection on the archived web as a source. The possible inclusion of web archives is weighed against establishing a collection oneself, the rapid changeability of the web is acknowledged, and the archiving form (screenshots and screen movies) and the archiving strategies (how to navigate a website while archiving) are clearly outlined, as are their consequences for the subsequent analysis.

4.1.3 Collecting and Integrating Sound and Web Pages

The previous two examples of web history focused on a visible web element, but there are also web histories that focus on sound on the web. The book chapter "Hearing the Past: The Sonic Web from MIDI to Music Streaming" (2018) by Jeremy Wade Morris traces the history of sound on the web, from early technologies that made it possible to play sounds, to streaming and podcasts. In addition to providing a historical overview of the development of web sound, the chapter dedicates a lot of attention to the challenges of collecting and using sound as a source.

As with all other web elements, sound on the web is subject to the ever-changing nature of the web, but collecting and preserving the web sounds of the past also involve some specific obstacles:

First, web archiving tools are primarily built on visual metaphors and thus neglect the role of audio. Second, preserving audio formats often requires preserving the sounds themselves as well as the technologies on which to play those sounds. Like so many other digital media, web audio is hard to hear not just because it is hard to find and save but because it is hard to know what to save along with it to make it playable in the future. (Morris, 2018, n.p.)

Thus, web historians may know how the web pages where a sound existed may have looked, but the sound itself is not retrievable. Or it may be retrievable, because some web archives, such as the Internet Archive, have large holdings of sound files, some of which were originally uploaded to the web, including songs, podcasts, and web radio. But these sound elements are preserved as audio files and not integrated with the web pages where they were initially placed, which leads Morris to conclude that "if the visual snapshots from the Wayback Machine are silent, the sound collections are barely visible." Because of web archiving traditions, one can either retrieve the web pages without the sound or the sound without the web pages.

In addition to the sounds that may have been saved because they existed as individual files, later in the history of the web, sound on the web—in particular, streaming—was disseminated with the specific aim of not being preservable.

The case of the history of web sound is a key example of the difficulties related to providing useful sources of specific web elements—either they were not collected, or they could not be replayed—just as it is an example of the general challenge of combining different bits and pieces of a web page, and in particular, as illustrated here, combining fragments originating in two different collections. Either the sound's context is available but not the sound element itself, or vice versa, and if both are available, assembling them may be a challenge.

4.1.4   Web Pages as Pictures—an Automated View

Like the previous three examples, the following example focuses on the visible (or audible) side when using the web of the past as a source for writing web history. However, it does this by employing an analytical method that, in fact, transforms the visible archived web based on HTML code into something with another digitality—an image with text recognition. In the article "The Rise and Fall of Text on the Web: A Quantitative Study of Web Archives" (Cocciolo, 2015), Anthony Cocciolo sets out to investigate how the quantity of one type of web element on web pages—written text—has developed over time. In brief, the aim of the study is to find out whether the use of text on the web has been declining, and if it has, when the decline started and to what extent it has occurred.

In a sense, this analysis is based on one source type, but with two different digital forms. What is analyzed is the quantity of text on the front pages of "six hundred captures of one hundred prominent and popular Webpages in the United States" (Cocciolo, 2015, p. 2) for the years 1999, 2002, 2005, 2008, 2011, and 2014. All these websites were queried in the Internet Archive by the use of a script, and their archive web addresses were retrieved. Then individual files of each of these URLs' web pages were created (using the Mozilla Firefox plugin "Grab Them All"). The next step was to automatically identify text in the images of the web pages from the Internet Archive, which was done by using a computer vision algorithm ("stroke width transform") that could detect text in images. The procedure makes it accessible as unicode text "by running the algorithm on the images of a Webpage to detect text regions, and then runs those regions through an optical character recognition process" (Cocciolo, 2015, p. 4). Finally, the information about the size of images and the percentage of text was exported to a database, and then it was analyzed (it showed that the percentage of text peaked in 2005, and has declined since then).

Cocciolo's study exemplifies how the digitality of the archived web in one form of web collection—the archived web as it is displayed in the Internet Archive's Wayback Machine—may be transformed into another form of archived web, a file with an image of the displayed web page. It also shows how this approach can be used to trace the development of written text on web pages, and showcases how images of web pages may be analyzed on a large scale. The transformation is from the archived web as assembled fragments into the archived web as an image, though an image that does not depict the online web as it was but that instead constitutes a rearchiving of what is already archived.

In his concluding remarks, Cocciolo briefly mentions another study that calculated the ratios between file types (text, image, audio), which indicates that the same research question could have been answered by studying the fragmented web as such—that is, by using the HTML code to calculate the number of specific file types, and even the number of words per page in the HTML code. But then, as Cocciolo notes, it could have been difficult to calculate the percentage of text relative to other web elements on the web page, just as text within images on the web page would not have been included.

In Cocciolo's study, the web pages in the Wayback Machine are used as they are displayed, without any reflection on their possible completeness and temporal inconsistencies (see sections 7.2 and 8.2), but given his analytical intent, digging more deeply into this may be irrelevant. In any case, this sort of "reverse engineering," from archived HTML to screen images with OCR, emphasizes how it is possible to interact with the archived web in ways that transform and reconstruct it through the research process, and that add potentially new applications of the archived web as well.

4.2   The Web Page

The web page is often an unacknowledged analytical unit, since it tends to either be an "invisible" context for analyses of web elements, or an unnoticed individual element in analyses of websites. However, all three examples that follow place the web page center stage, and each retains a focus on the visible web.

4.2.1 Web Page Design

In the journal article "Digital Style History: The Development of Graphic Design on the Internet" (Engholm, 2002), Ida Engholm sets out to study the, at the time relatively new, phenomenon of web design. Her aims are to develop an analytical approach to web design as an aesthetic phenomenon, inspired by the art history concept of "style," and to present a brief outline of the historical development of web design with a graphic-aesthetic focus. According to Engholm, this history is characterized by two main approaches, "a pragmatic, functionalistic approach" and an "avant-garde orientation, not caring much about transmission speed, functionality, and user friendliness" (Engholm, 2002, p. 198).

In analyzing these two approaches, Engholm presents a number of examples of web pages in the form of images, and each comes with the full original web address, as a clickable link, and with a "Last revised" date. Apparently, the analyzed web pages were archived as screenshots by the author (a similar archiving form was used for the collection in the Danish Webmuseum (webmuseum.dk) that is based on the findings in Engholm's doctoral dissertation (Engholm, 2003)). Also, in some cases, only web addresses are mentioned, without any image documentation.

Engholm's study illustrates the changeability of the online web and some of the limitations associated with this, when web history is based on self-archiving by the web historian and not on material in a web archive. Of the 13 hyperlinks in the article, 6 were still working in 2017 but with present-day content, 6 were no longer online, and only one displayed the content that was online in 2002 when the article was published (in fact, the content as it looked in 1995). Thus, although (some of) the archived web pages could be seen in the article, several could not, and today they may be available only in a web archive if at all. However, the study also illustrates that finding old web material on the World "Wild" Web is still possible (see section 6.7).

Screenshots were chosen as a way of archiving, which is a nice fit with Engholm's focus on visual aesthetics, but she includes no reflection on archiving forms and strategies, probably because collecting and preserving the web material is not considered web archiving at all. The lack of information about how and why the web pages were preserved bears witness to an immediate approach to web preservation. Since the web pages are still online at the time of writing, and its rapid changes have not been thematized.

4.2.2   News and Visual Design across Media

The visual presentation of web pages is also the topic of Lynne Cooke's article, "A Visual Convergence of Print, Television, and the Internet: Charting 40 Years of Design Change in News Presentation" (Cooke, 2005). However, her scope and approach are broader than the aesthetics of web design, since she investigates their development with the aim of examining "how specific designs form and migrate across media over time" (Cooke, 2005, p. 23). Thus, the development of the web's visual design is examined from the overarching perspective of media history, with a focus on how visual design migrates among media, including newspapers from 1960 to 2002, television news from 1968 and 2000, and the web in 1990–2002. Thus, this is not only a study of the development of web design, but also of the design of the web, compared to that of other media types. The study includes five newspapers, seven television news programs, and twelve news websites, and for the websites, the focus is on the front page (80 news website front pages were studied). Regarding the web pages, Cooke discusses whether news web sites have "followed a visual evolutionary path similar to newspaper layout due to advances in technology" (Cooke, 2005, p. 23). With regard to the source used, the author clearly states her reason for choosing news as the genre for the study: "The news was chosen as a genre for longitudinal visual analysis because of its existence and archival availability in three visual media, and because the news is a public commodity" (Cooke, 2005, p. 23).

The foregoing considerations also hold for the web, since what is studied is material from the Internet Archive. However, Cooke acknowledges that unlike what exists for newspapers and television, "there is no comprehensive archive of news websites," and she continues,

In addition, the irregular holdings and content of the public web archive, the Way-Back Machine (www.web.archive.org/collections/web.html), resulted in a purposive sample that was largely based on availability. News website home pages included for analysis were selected according to their completeness (all textual and pictorial elements). To maintain sampling consistency across media, home pages from Saturdays and Sundays were not included in the sample. (Cooke, 2005, p. 28)

Cooke's study is an early example of the use of an existing web archive for a web history study. The study does not mention the possibility of using archived material from sources other than a web archive, such as the news websites themselves or the author's own web archiving (if such exists); instead, a web archive appears to be the obvious choice. The reasons for this may be that the Internet Archive's Wayback Machine is now available, and that the cross-media analytical purpose has already directed attention to existing collections of old media. The latter may also be the reason that the study in general reflects on the quality of the source material. In the case of the archived web, it reveals an awareness that the chosen collection comes with some shortcomings, since concerns such as irregular archiving intervals and incompleteness are explicitly addressed, which is why the study has to be based on what was available.

4.2.3 Screencast Documentary

In 2008 Richard Rogers issued a short video titled *Google and the Politics of Tabs*, which narrates the historical changes that had taken place on the front page of Google from 1998 to 2007. In terms of genre, the video was labeled a "screencast documentary," inspired by the video *Heavy Metal Umlaut*, produced in 2005 by software developer Jon Udell (Udell, 2005a). Udell's video is about the changes made to the *Wikipedia* page "Heavy Metal Umlaut" (a page about the use of an umlaut in the names of heavy metal bands), and it was produced on the basis of the online web, a procedure made possible because *Wikipedia* tracks the historical changes made to any given page. In contrast, *Google and the Politics of Tabs* was made with the use of archived web pages from the Internet Archive:

Colleagues and I captured the historical pages of a URL (Google.com's, during what was its tenth anniversary, too). We compiled the unique pages (the ones with an * next to them in the Wayback Machine's results page), loaded them in a slide show, and played them back in the style of time-lapse photography, or screencast documentary, with a voiceover track telling the history of Google from the changes to its interface from 1998 to 2007. (Rogers, 2013, p. 10; see also pp. 68–69)

This screencast documentary was followed by several videos of the same type (see Rogers, 2017, pp. 165–166, for examples), and the practical aspects of this way of narrating web history were later systematized and supported by tools and techniques (developed by the Digital Methods Initiative at the University of Amsterdam) (Rogers, 2017, p. 166).

Google and the Politics of Tabs demonstrates how the archived web in a web archive may (also) be used to narrate the web history of one web page (and of any other web stratum, for that matter), and the video and supporting tools showcase how this may be done. The short video format does not allow for any reflection on the source material's completeness or temporal inconsistency, which is why such reflection must be published elsewhere (the ephemerality of the web and the affordances of the Wayback Machine as a research tool—including the temporal inconsistencies when clicking links—are discussed in Rogers, 2013, pp. 61–81, and Rogers, 2017).

4.3   The Website

The website is the web stratum on which most web history studies have focused. This section presents several examples of history written with the web as a source, and a number of histories of the web where the focus is either on the visible or the hidden web, or on both.

4.3.1   History with the Web

The inclusion of websites as a historical source in studies of topics outside of the web itself started to emerge around 2014–2015. An example of this is an article by Sophie Gebeil about collective memory related to North African immigration, based on 100 websites from the French web archived between 2000 and 2013 ("Le web, nouvel espace de mobilization des mémoires marginales: Les mémoires de l'immigration maghrébine sur l'internet français (2000–2013)" (Gebeil, 2015b; the article is a preparatory work for her dissertation, *La fabrique numérique des mémoires de l'immigration maghrébine sur le web français (1999–2014)* (Gebeil, 2015a)). After having outlined some of the challenges that the internet in general poses for historiography, including the rapid changing of the web (Gebeil, 2015b, p. 132), Gebeil emphasizes that the internet, and in particular the archived web, is a legitimate and very useful historical source for studies of contemporary society: "The internet constitutes important historical documentation when studying collective memory and the use of the past. Thus, the existence of web archives has determined my methodological choices to a large extent" (Gebeil, 2015b, p. 132, my translation).

Gebeil's study builds primarily on websites provided by the two national French web archives, at the INA (Institut National de l'Audiovisuel) and the BNF (Bibliothèque Nationale de France), but archived websites are supplemented with interviews with web users. Despite the fact that large portions of the French cultural heritage on the web have been collected and preserved, and that the study could not have been conducted if it were not for the holdings of the two web archives, Gebeil notes that both web archives have their limitations when it comes to how well they represent the French web and that they come with a number of biases: "So far, the entire French web domain has not been archived in its totality, the quality of the archive is uneven, the absence of data is a consequence of the archiving frequency" (Gebeil, 2015b, pp. 134–135, my translation).

Another important lesson learned from this study is that close collaborations with the web archives have proved important at several stages of the research process, including when searching the material, when suggesting that online material not in the archive be archived, and in relation to the development of digital tools to unlock the material by identifying file formats and by data mining (Gebeil, 2015b, p. 135).

Gebeil's study clearly shows that the web is an indispensable historical source when studying topics other than the web itself (in this case, memories of immigration), it demonstrates a high degree of understanding of the archived web's digitality, and, finally, it makes clear that the archived web need not be the only source used. It also emphasizes that the holdings of web archives partly determine what may be studied, and that researchers' close collaboration with web archives helps improve the collections and facilitates better research.

Since 2014 there have been a number of British research projects using the archived web as a historical source to write history with the web, based mainly on the "JISC UK Web Domain Dataset (1996–2013)."[2] Within the framework of the research project "Big UK Domain Data for the Arts and Humanities (BUDDAH)" (buddah.projects.history.ac.uk), the JISC data set was used as a stepping-stone to studies of a great variety of topics, including Beat literature, British Euroskepticism, and commemoration of World War II (for an overview of these projects, see Cowls, 2017).

Several of the above-mentioned studies focus on the website as an analytical unit, including Rowan Aust's study of how the content of the BBC's website changed over time in response to the sexual abuse allegations against the broadcaster Jimmy Savile (Aust, 2014). When setting out to uncover how the BBC is "treating the online presence of Savile" and how "the Web Archive [can] be used to examine this" (Aust, 2014, p. 3), Aust compares archived material from before the scandal with material on the online web, and her conclusion is that changes have been made to the BBC website. However, as she demonstrates by consulting the BBC's editorial guidelines, *Removal of BBC Online Content*, it is clear that "the BBC

Online News site is intended as a permanent archive" (Aust, 2014, p. 8). This study exemplifies how the archived web may be used as a historical source together with the online web, and that the online web is by no means a reliable archive, even in cases where one might expect it to be.

4.3.2   Web History with and of the Web

Before considering other examples of web history as the history of web-sites, it is worth mentioning a study that clearly situates itself at the nexus of web history with the web and of the web. In the article "Reconstruct-ing a Website's Lost Past: Methodological Issues Concerning the History of Unibo.it" (Nanni, 2017) Federico Nanni has two aims. The first is to ana-lyze the development of the University of Bologna's main website, unibo.it, including methodological reflection on how this may be done. The second is to argue that the archived web can "give us new and distinct insights into the recent past of academic institutions," thus "highlighting its useful-ness for the communities that study academic institutions" (Nanni, 2017, pp. 5, 6).

The major challenge for Nanni's project is that Italy does not have a national web archive; as he notes, "no project with the specific purpose of preserving the Italian web-sphere exists" (Nanni, 2017, p. 10). There is only one crawl of the .it web domain from 2006 and another crawl of the PhD dissertation repositories of Italian universities. Thus, the project had to rely on a variety of other source types, including library and archive materials, interviews, newspapers and forums, and both the online web (Nanni, 2017, pp. 25–32) and the archived web, so the unibo.it website was searched for in the Internet Archive and in other national web archives. However, unibo. it was apparently not available in the Internet Archive, but on the assump-tion that this could not be true, Nanni painstakingly set out to determine what had happened (together with the Internet Archive and CeSIA, the team that had recently supervised unibo.it). This led to some clarifications concerning an old robots.txt file, and in 2015 unibo.it became available in the Internet Archive's Wayback Machine, as it appeared that the material had actually been archived for the last 15 years (Nanni, 2017, pp. 60–65).[3] As to material in national web archives outside Italy, some material from unibo.it was located that had probably been archived unintentionally, because the web crawler had followed hyperlinks on an archived web page that pointed to unibo.it.

Nanni's study of unibo.it highlights a number of relevant methodological-cal issues and lessons learned about the use of the archived web as a source. It illustrates the advantages of including a variety of sources in addition to the archived web. It also shows that though web archives may initially appear incomplete, a more thorough inspection may reveal that the relevant material is still there. This emphasizes that web archives may not only be opaque to a researcher; in particular, large-scale crawled web collections are so for the web archives as well, because it is impossible to get a complete overview of the collection. Furthermore, the fact that it is difficult for the web archive and for the researcher to determine the exact contents of the archive underlines the importance of close collaboration between these two actors. The porous nature of the borders of crawled web collections is also illustrated—that is, the fact that a web archive's web archivists do not know exactly what happens once the web crawlers are let loose on the web, with the possible positive result that a national web archive may have collected material relevant to researchers elsewhere (see section 5.3.2 about web crawling). Finally, Nanni's study clearly attests to the challenges of reconstructing a website based on holdings in other web collections.

4.3.3   Web Histories of Websites

In what follows, examples of histories of websites are presented, first histories focusing on the visible side, then examples focusing on the hidden web and on combinations of the visible and the hidden.

A typical example of an analysis of the visible side of a website is Albrecht Hofheinz's study of the history of the allah.com website (Hofheinz, 2010). In terms of sources, this study builds primarily on material from the Internet Archive. However, other sources are also included, such as "'live' interaction and private archiving, chiefly in 2003, 2005 and 2008, supplemented by common web tools such as whois or Alexa," but interviews are excluded, "in an attempt to demonstrate the extent (and thereby also the limits) of what can be found out using only online sources" (Hofheinz, 2010, p. 106). Some methodological challenges related to the use of the archived web as a source are also discussed—for instance, the rapid and frequent changes to websites and the fact that "not only the Internet Archive but any archive has always had many more holes than content" (Hofheinz, 2010, p. 106).

Other examples of studies of the visible side of websites that are based on the Internet Archive's collections, and that also include several source types, are Michael Stevenson's article "Rethinking the Participatory Web: A History of Hotwired's 'New Publishing Paradigm,' 1994–1997" (Stevenson, 2016), which examines the history of the website *HotWired*, *Wired* magazine's web-only publication, launched in 1994; Sybil Nolan's chapter "Born Outside the Newsroom: The Creation of the Age Online" (Nolan, 2017), which explores the 1995 creation of Age Online, the first major newspaper website in Australia; and the book chapter "The Changing Digital Faces of Science Museums: A Diachronic Analysis of Museum Websites" by Anwesha Chakraborty and Federico Nanni (Chakraborty & Nanni, 2017), which investigates the historical development of three science museums' websites. Stevenson supplements material from the Internet Archive with interviews (Stevenson, 2016, p. 1332); Nolan draws on the archive of the newspaper *The Age*, corporate reports, and her own experience working as a journalist for the newspaper, in addition to using the Internet Archive and interviews (Nolan, 2017, pp. 109, 116); and Chakraborty and Nanni base their study on the Internet Archive, interviews, and the live web (Chakraborty & Nanni, 2017, p. 160). None of these studies addresses the question of the possible temporal inconsistency of web pages and websites viewed through the Wayback Machine, which I discuss later (section 7.2), probably with good reason, since they are not particularly time sensitive, although the embedded temporal inconsistency on the page level is bound to be a concern.

All the foregoing studies of the visible side of websites indicate that the Internet Archive tends to be the standard web archive to turn to in these types of cases, but that it may be supplemented by a variety of other source types.

The following two examples are studies that still retain a focus on the website as the analytical unit, but do so by studying the hidden side, the HTML code, and not what may actually be seen on the website.

In the chapter "Live *versus* Archive: Comparing a Web Archive to a Population of Web Pages," Hale et al. take the rapid changes of the online web as a starting point for asking "How good are the archival data?" (Hale et al., 2017, p. 45). This question is examined by studying one website—tripadvisor. co.uk—as it is archived in two different collections, the Internet Archive and a collection from the online web made by the researchers themselves. The case is narrowed to focus on all tourist attractions in London listed on TripAdvisor's website, and the material from the Internet Archive was provided via the "JISC UK Web Domain Dataset (1996–2013)" (see above). The researcher-generated collection from the online web and the material from the Internet Archive were analyzed as HTML code (Hale et al., 2017, p. 51), and, as for the latter, not as seen through the Wayback Machine. Hale et al. conclude that the archival coverage is very heterogeneous, and that

there is a clear bias toward prominent, well-known and highly-rated web pages. Smaller, less well-known and lower-rated web pages are less likely to be archived. It is worth noting that all the archived data we used came from the Internet Archive; so, the archived data are probably the best, most complete source possible for this time period but it is clearly not complete, and it contains significant biases. (Hale et al., 2017, p. 59)

Hale et al. address one of the core concerns related to studying the digitality of the archived web, namely, the extent of its completeness, compared to what was once online (see section 7.1.2). This is done by providing detailed information on the expected incompleteness of web archives, and by studying the HTML code by the use of digital tools, instead of focusing on the visible web as seen via the Wayback Machine.

Another study based on the "JISC UK Web Domain Dataset (1996–2013)" is Josh Cowls and Jonathan Bright's book chapter, "International Hyperlinks in Online News Media" (Cowls & Bright, 2017). This chapter investigates the outlinking patterns on the BBC News website, with a particular focus on the countries in which the websites that are linked to are located. Hyperlinks were extracted from the JISC data set and filtered to include only hyperlinks emerging from the BBC's website (Cowls & Bright, 2017, p. 107). Two variables were identified, based on this data: first, information about where hyperlinks pointed to was obtained from the BBC's website (other country-specific web domains), and second, information in the text of the hyperlink was analyzed, to find indications of what the news article on the web page was about and which countries were mentioned. Thus, the textual hyperlink information was used as a proxy for the body text that was not available in the data set.

Cowls and Bright's study illustrates how the hidden HTML code may be used to analyze the connectedness of one individual website, by looking at outgoing links only. This way of using hyperlink information is different from carrying out a hyperlink network analysis where the mutual linkages between websites are analyzed (see below). It also exemplifies how hyperlinks not only contain information about where they point to, but in some cases also include textual information that may be used as a proxy for the text on the web page.

Finally, I present two examples of histories of a website, now focusing on the visible and invisible sides of the websites.

In "The Online Development of the Ministry of Defence (MoD) and Armed Forces" (Raffal, 2014), Harry Raffal explores the development of the websites related to Britain's armed forces—that is, the army, navy, air force, and Ministry of Defence. The study is based on material from the Internet Archive and from the "JISC UK Web Domain Dataset (1996–2013)," and it approached the websites in two different ways. On the one hand, the content on web pages as seen through the Wayback Machine was analyzed, including visual design and navigational elements; on the other hand, a hyperlink network analysis was performed, to investigate the link structure in which the websites were situated. Among the many important methodological reflections in the study, three are particularly worth noting in the present context. First, the websites to be included in the study "were selected by organization rather than URL, as in the case of the Royal Navy and MoD websites the primary URL changed during the course of this period" (Raffal, 2014 p. 1). Second, it was difficult to evaluate the material on web pages with missing web elements, which "raised the question of whether incomplete captures should be disregarded and the nearest complete site iteration used instead" (Raffal, 2014 p. 3). Third, it is showcased how, although a given web page as seen in the Wayback Machine might appear almost empty, the underlying HTML code could be used to trace missing elements and to provide valuable information about the web page:

The analysis of websites in the initial corpus used complete captures if they had unchanged content, determined by inspecting the underlying code; otherwise the incomplete iteration was used. Incomplete captures can have significant value, often yielding data from remaining coded elements or in descriptions and annotations applied to content, particularly navigational elements or images. Captures of sites which record only an error message or a holding page because the site is down can also yield data. (Raffal, 2014, p. 3)

Raffal's study shows how a focus on both the visible and hidden sides of a website may be combined, and it illustrates the uncertainty associated with using the URL as a consistent identifier for a website over time, since the URL for a given organization may change (see section 9.2). The challenge

posed by missing web elements is also debated and—most importantly—
the usefulness of using a web page's HTML code to shed light on missing
elements is foregrounded (this is what is termed a web philology approach
in section 9.2).

In contrast to Raffal's study, where attention to the visible and hidden
sides of the websites is divided almost evenly, the pendulum swings toward
the code level in Ian Milligan's book chapter, "Welcome to the Web: The
Online Community of Geocities during the Early Years of the World Wide
Web" (Milligan, 2017), and the visible web is treated differently than in a
close analysis of individual web pages.

Milligan studies GeoCities, one of the first large-scale virtual communities, which was not only used by people with an interest in computers; it
was divided into neighborhoods, such as "Athens," for users interested in
education, teaching, and reading, or the "EnchantedForest," for children.
The study is based on the GeoCities data set archived by the Archive Team,
combined with material archived by the Internet Archive (Milligan, 2017,
p. 140; see also section 6.4), and after having observed that "we cannot read
every single page, or even a reasonable sample of them" (Milligan, 2017,
p. 148), Milligan turned to digitally supported methods. Computational
methods were used to investigate how cohesive the web pages are within
a neighborhood—for instance, whether "Athens" is actually about education, teaching, and reading, or whether the "EnchantedForest" is actually
for children. First, the text of the web pages was analyzed by the use of topic
modeling; second, every image from each neighborhood was extracted and
arranged in montages of thousands of images with enabled zoom in/out,
thus providing access to large amounts of data while shifting between distant and close reading (in both cases, neighborhoods appeared cohesive)
(Milligan, 2017, pp. 148–149). Computational methods were also used to
analyze descriptions of community leaders (presented in a word cloud),
images of awards, texts of guest books, and the link network of guest books.
In the conclusion, when debating what would have further promoted this
type of research, Milligan notes:

As the Internet Archive prepares to re-launch their Wayback Machine in 2017 with
some form of full-text search, this kind of research will become more accessible.
However, access to the underlying WebARChive (ARC and WARC) files that comprise these holdings would be essential to facilitate the sort of research done on
GeoCities in this chapter at scale. (Milligan, 2017, p. 157)

Milligan's study showcases the benefits of using a variety of different computational methods to unlock large amounts of the archived web, and ways of integrating distant and close reading other than the Wayback Machine are explored, such as an image montage that allows for shifting between the two modes. Finally, the study emphasizes that providing researchers with access to the archiving files holding the archived content is crucial if their use of web archives is to take the next steps (see section 8.2).

4.4   The Web Sphere

The following examples are all web sphere histories, either histories with the web, based on a study of the hidden web, or histories of the web, where the focus is on both the visible and the hidden web.

4.4.1   Histories with a Web Sphere

What follows are examples of histories of a given topic with a related archived web sphere as their source. If the hidden side of the web sphere is analyzed, and if the web sphere is to be studied on a large scale, some sort of digital tool or other digital-based approach is often needed to provide the corpus to be studied, as illustrated in the following four examples.

In the book chapter "Using the Web to Examine the Evolution of the Abortion Debate in Australia, 2005–2015" (Ackland & Evans, 2017), Robert Ackland and Ann Evans ask what we can "learn about the evolution of the abortion debate in Australia over the past ten years using data from the World Wide Web" (Ackland & Evans, 2017, p. 159). The study sets out to answer the question by analyzing the hyperlink network and the website text on websites related to the abortion question in Australia. The study is not based on an existing web archive, but on a collection established by the authors themselves, in 2005 and 2015. Based on the results of a Google query, the hyperlink and website text was collected in both years through the use of dedicated software (the VOSON software that incorporates a web crawler) (Ackland & Evans, 2017, pp. 165, 170). When concluding the chapter, Ackland and Evans debate the challenges of using web archive material in this type of study:

In order to construct large-scale hyperlink networks from web archives, it is necessary that these archives allow crawlers or else provide publicly available application programming interfaces (API) so that the hyperlink network data can be programmatically extracted at scale. There does not exist an Australian web archive with such capabilities and hence, we could not have conducted the research presented in this chapter without having crawled the live web at both time points (2005 and 2015), that is, effectively creating a purpose-built archive of hyperlink and website text data. Thus, historical hyperlink network analysis typically requires researchers to collect snapshots from the live web over time. (Ackland & Evans, 2017, p. 189)

In a 2012 article, "Newspapers and the Long-Term Implications of Hyperlinking" (Weber, 2012), Matthew S. Weber investigates organizational networks over time in the news media community in the United States, from 1999 to 2006. The study analyzes the development of hyperlink networks on a selection of news websites, based on material from the Internet Archive. Since hyperlinks are not easily extracted on a large scale from the Internet Archive, the author used a custom-built web crawler to crawl and extract the data from the archive:

Data crawling and extraction was conducted using a custom Web crawler, History-Crawl, designed specifically to interface with the Internet Archive and extract hyperlink data from Web pages over time. The program allows users to input a number of parameters, including a seed sample of uniform resource locators (URLs), years to be sampled and the number of steps outward to be crawled. (Weber, 2012, p. 192)

In the book chapter "Religious Discourse in the Archived Web: Rowan Williams, Archbishop of Canterbury, and the Sharia Law Controversy of 2008" (Webster, 2017a), Peter Webster sets out to study the place of Islam in British politics and society, with the sharia law controversy of 2008 as a focal point, to explore how the archived web may be used to shed new light on this case, among other things. Webster's study uses the previously mentioned "JISC UK Web Domain Dataset (1996–2013)" (including the Host Link Graph), which was based on data extracted from the web material on the .uk web domain from the Internet Archive. Utilizing this material, the project focuses on "host-to-host relations as a proxy measure of attention paid by the individual or organization by whom the linking host is controlled" (Webster, 2017a, p. 193). However, the Host Link Graph was not studied in its entirety; only relevant hyperlinks were extracted.

Finally, in a book chapter titled "Exploring the Memory of the First World War Using Web Archives: Web Graphs Seen from Different Angles" (Beaudouin et al., 2018), Beaudouin et al. use the archived web as a source for an exploratory study that is part of a larger project about how digital sources could support studies of the memory of World War I on its centenary. The aim of the exploratory analysis is to "understand how the memory of the war is socially organised on the web using hyperlink networks" (Beaudouin et al., 2018, n.p.), including investigating how to extract and visualize hyperlink information from web archives.

Beaudouin et al.'s analysis is based on an already established special collection on the centenary of World War I, in the web archive at the Bibliothèque Nationale de France (BNF). Two types of derived data were studied—hyperlinks and descriptive metadata from the selection tool that was initially used when the special collection was created—rather than the archived files (see sections 7.2 and 8.2 about metadata files). The hyperlink data relevant to the analysis were extracted from metadata files in WAT format (Beaudouin et al., 2018, n.p.).

Each of the last four examples demonstrates in its own way various approaches to the same challenge, namely, how a historical study with an archived web sphere as a source, focused on studying the hidden web on a large scale, may provide access to substantial amounts of the archived web in a form suitable for these types of studies, and thereby create a useful corpus for study. Ackland and Evans proceed by archiving the web themselves with the use of dedicated archiving software instead of using a web collection, Weber had a custom tool created that allows for the retrieval of relevant material in an online web archive, Webster uses an already established derived data set, and Beaudouin et al. had access to metadata of an existing web archive, which permitted them to create the corpus they wanted to study from within the web archive. Each of the solutions comes with limitations. Creating one's own collection is not possible retroactively, and using an automated tool to access an online web archive from the outside may not always be allowed by the web archive and may require prior agreement. Moreover, relevant and useful derived data sets must be established, and the web archive must provide researcher access to WAT files and the curators' selection tool. In brief, this resonates with Milligan's wish, mentioned above, for researcher access to the archived files, and it exemplifies the great variety of possible forms of access and needs, depending on the research project.

4.4.2 Histories of Web Spheres

Not only did Kirsten A. Foot and Steven M. Schneider coin the term *web sphere* in their book *Web Campaigning* (Foot & Schneider, 2006), the book itself also constitutes the first example of an analysis of a web sphere, in this case focusing on the visible side of the web. In *Web Campaigning* the authors analyze how the use of the web in political campaigns in the United States developed between 2000, 2002, and 2004, and in particular, they focus on how voters were informed, supporters became involved, users and political actors became connected, and advocates were mobilized (Foot & Schneider, 2006, p. 24).

Foot and Schneider's study is based on a range of types of source material, including interviews, focus groups, surveys, and data from web producers and web users (Foot & Schneider, 2006, pp. 42, 211–225). But the archived web in its visible form was also analyzed, and it constitutes an important source for the study. The archived web was presented in various ways. First, in an exploratory study in 2000 the authors themselves archived the relevant web sphere (1999–2000) from the online web. Second, with this collection as a stepping-stone, they established a collaboration with the US Library of Congress, with a view to collecting and preserving the web sphere related to elections in 2002 and 2004 (Foot & Schneider, 2006, p. 42; cf. also Foot & Schneider, 2010, pp. 62–63, for extended information about this collaboration).[4] They also used websites archived by the Internet Archive and the Annenberg 2000 Election Web Archive (Foot & Schneider, 2006, p. 239). In addition, when coding the archived websites to prepare them for analysis, "coders used the WebArchivist Resource Coder, which enabled distributed, Web-based coding and coordination of resources to be coded" (Foot & Schneider, 2006, p. 215). Finally, Foot and Schneider reflect on how archived websites should be referenced, "using archival URLs when possible" (Foot & Schneider, 2006, p. 43).

Foot and Schneider's study highlights the advantages of establishing collaborations between researchers and an archiving institution to build a collection that fits a specific research project, and, as is the case here, a collection that is also useful (and accessible) to other researchers. But as was often seen in the early days of web history writing, creating a collection on one's own was the starting point, and this collection had to be combined with other collections. This was probably not as big a challenge in this case, because the hidden side of the archived web was not used—for instance, no automated hyperlink analysis of the connecting patterns of users and political actors was made. Also, the authors relied on what is probably the first digital tool to help code and analyze the archived web, and they offered suggestions on the most feasible referencing practices.

Each of the next four cases is an example of histories of web spheres, focused on the hidden web, where the web sphere is delimited by the borders of a nation, thereby defining the web sphere as whatever relates to a given nation. However, the four examples have different focal points.

In a journal article, "Where Do Bloggers Blog? Platform Transitions within the Historical Dutch Blogosphere" (Weltevrede and Helmond, 2012), Esther Weltevrede and Anne Helmond map the historical changes in the Dutch blogosphere from 1999 to 2009. Based on an initial list of Dutch blogging URLs (originating from an early Dutch blogosphere index), material was retrieved from the Internet Archive, and a colink analysis of the hyperlink network was performed, year by year. They also determined the countries from which blogs originated (by querying for ccTLD), and which software platform was used by the bloggers. In each case, digital tools—in some cases custom software—were used to perform the analysis. The authors conclude:

URLs are very rich sources of information often following a certain syntax, which makes them very suitable for analysis. Here we used URL analysis in two ways: TLD analysis and platform analysis. With source code analysis we contribute to the study of software in general and, more specifically, the study of national software. The method developed provides insight into the software powering a blogosphere. (Weltevrede & Helmond, 2012, n.p.)

The study of the development of the Dutch blogosphere shows how much information may be pulled out of one small piece of code, the hyperlink, just as it emphasizes that digital methods and custom software are needed to unpack large amounts of archived web code.

A national blogosphere may be considered a subsphere within a larger national web space, a national web sphere. The question of how a national web sphere may be reconstructed on the basis of the archived web is the topic of the book chapter "Probing a Nation's Web Domain: A New Approach to Web History and a New Kind of Historical Source" (Brügger, 2017b), and of a number of chapters in the edited volume *The Historical Web and Digital Humanities: The Case of National Web Domains* (Brügger & Laursen, 2018). Brügger (2017b) debates how the borders of a national web sphere may be drawn in terms of space and time. He also outlines what an analysis of a national web sphere may focus on when analyzing the web code, including size in bytes, geolocation of websites, hyperlink networks and outgoing hyperlinks from the national domain, how often the websites are updated, file types, software types, language, and modeling of topics (Brügger, 2017b, pp. 67–71). Brügger and Laursen (2018) dedicate a number of chapters to addressing the challenge of reconstructing a national web sphere, not by identifying its outer limits, but by combining the patchwork of different subnational collections, as is the case in the United Kingdom, where "there is no single archive of the .uk country code Top Level Domain (ccTLD). Rather there are many archives, which overlap and diverge in multiple and still largely unexplored ways" (Winters, 2018, n.p.). Instead, in the Netherlands "several provincial and municipal archives started with local web archiving projects," whereby "significant parts of the Dutch web were preserved through all these ... collections, which were many times small, local projects with limited budgets and resources" (Teszelszky, 2018, n.p.), or in Belgium, where no national web archive exists, but nevertheless, "even though the Belgian web is currently not systematically archived, through initial desk research a number of existing web-archiving initiatives in Belgium have been uncovered" (Chambers & Mechant, 2018, n.p.).

The above-mentioned studies are examples of how a large national corpus may be delimited in space and time, and how such a corpus may be reconstructed on the basis of several (possibly) overlapping local, regional, and national web archives.

The following three studies also focus on the history of a national web sphere, but in contrast to the above-mentioned ones, each builds on a variety of other web-related metadata, from the online web and from web archives.

In the article "What Does the Web Remember of Its Deleted Past? An Archival Reconstruction of the Former Yugoslav Top-Level Domain" (Ben-David, 2016), Anat Ben-David sets out to reconstruct the history of the country-code top-level web domain of Yugoslavia, .yu, which was deleted from the internet in 2010. No national web archive ever existed for Yugoslavia, so the starting point of the study was four lists of historical URLs in the .yu domain that the author succeeded in obtaining from other sources. Based on these, the Internet Archive was queried to find the URLs' websites and the HTML code was saved. Then links were stripped from these web pages and the links pointing to another .yu domain were preserved, which was done in five iterations; all the above steps were handled by custom software (Ben-David, 2016, p. 1109). Thus, this exploratory hyperlink analysis expanded the number of .yu web domains found, thereby expanding the corpus to be studied.

A somewhat similar approach to the foregoing is described by Marta Musso and Francesco Merletti in the article "This Is the Future: A Reconstruction of the UK Business Web Space (1996–2001)" (Musso & Merletti, 2016). Musso and Merletti reconstruct the UK business web space that existed between 1996 and 2001, including how many British companies first created a website and which business sectors were most likely to do so. The corpus studied was created based on historical web directories about business, similar to the "Yahoo! Business Directory" and the "Yahoo! Regional Business Directory." First, the SHINE search interface was used to query the "JISC UK Web Domain Dataset (1996–2013)" for URLs to business directories, then these URLs were found in and retrieved from the Internet Archive, stored in a database, and used to search Whois databases and the Internet Archive for companies' websites (Musso & Merletti, 2016, pp. 1123–1124); all steps were facilitated by various custom software.

In "Exploring the Domain Names of the Danish Web" (Brügger et al., 2017), Brügger et al. conduct a preparatory study for a broader analysis of the development of the national Danish web between 2005 and 2015. In this study, the archived web, as found in the Internet Archive, is compared to another type of web metadata, namely the complete list of national web domains, which in Denmark's case is the .dk country-code top-level domain (ccTLD). The lists of all the Danish domain names registered year by year may be found in the Danish national web archive, Netarkivet, where they serve as seed lists for web crawls of the entire .dk ccTLD (Brügger et al., 2017, p. 63). These lists were analyzed to map the development of domain names on the Danish web, followed by a comparison of the domain name lists to the number of domains actually archived in Netarkivet and in the Internet Archive; in all steps, software-supported methods were used. The aim of these analyses was to determine whether domain name lists could be used as a historical source in their own right, and to execute a large-scale evaluation of the (in)completeness of a web archive, namely, an entire ccTLD (each year was highly variable with respect to how much of the Danish web was archived in Netarkivet and in the Internet Archive).

The foregoing three cases are examples of how web metadata, such as lists of URLs, may be studied either individually or in combination with collections of the archived web. In the latter case, lists of URLs may be used as a stepping-stone to creating a corpus from a web collection, for instance in combination with an exploratory use of hyperlink analyses (cf. also Weltevrede & Helmond, 2012), or testing the completeness of a web collection on a large scale, the same aim that Hale et al. pursued above, but on a ccTLD level, in contrast to that of the individual website. What is also illustrated is the need for custom digital tools and scripts to unlock large amounts of the archived web.

4.5   The Web as a Whole

The web as a whole is a phenomenon that transcends the other strata. This section presents three examples that explore this, illustrated by histories of the web browser, of global hyperlink networks, and of Google's search algorithm, with a focus on both the visible and the hidden web.

In the book chapter "Browsers and Browser Wars" (Weber, 2018), Marc Weber provides a historical overview of the window into the web—the web browser—from Tim Berners-Lee's first browser-editor and line-mode browsers to the graphical user interface browsers later produced for other platforms. Since the web browser is the software and textual device that interprets the HTML code and packages the web content to become a readable web page to appear in a browser window, it is not part of the web archiving process itself. The web browser is something one looks through to access the web, and therefore it tends to be overlooked, and if preserved, this is mainly done by accident, because web pages were preserved as screenshots. Thus, this type of study often has to rely on screenshots of the web as seen in old browsers and preserved in the past, to be found on the World "Wild" Web, for example (see section 6.7).

In the article "Structural Changes in the 2003–2009 Global Hyperlink Network" (Park et al., 2011), Park et al. extend network analysis beyond national borders by studying the development of the global hyperlink network from 2003 to 2009. The study is based on data on hyperlinks retrieved by querying search engines:

An input file that listed a set of search queries to retrieve webpages (ending with .uk) sending at least one link to webpages (ending with .kr) was made. For example, Yahoo's search command to search for webpages linking from the UK to South Korea was as follows: "linkdomain: .KR site: .UK." Then the input file was automatically sent to Yahoo by using LexiURL Searcher, a social science web analysis tool. (Park et al., 2011, p. 527)

Queries along these lines were performed in 2003 and 2009, using Alta-Vista and Yahoo, respectively, since at the time they were the only search engines providing interlinked information. Thus, the data for this study originates in a type of "web archive" usually not considered a web archive at all, namely, the database of a search engine (since Yahoo acquired Alta-Vista, the same database was used in 2003 and 2009; Park et al., 2011, p. 527). However, the use of a database of this nature also implies that the searches had to have been made in the past, which in this case was done as part of a 2003 study that was not looking at development, but was then replicated in 2009; this raises the question of the extent to which the two data sets are comparable.

Search engines have become an inherent part of the web, and they cut across all types of web strata. In chapter 5 of her dissertation, *Repurposing Digital Methods: The Research Affordances of Platforms and Engines* (Welte-vrede, 2016, pp. 101–130), Esther Weltevrede examines the historical development of Google's search algorithm. For obvious reasons, the algorithms are not available as such, which is why Weltevrede decided to study the effects of the algorithms with a view to finding out "what can be known by using the search engine as a research device" (Weltevrede, 2016, p. 130). For instance, this approach was used in connection with results pages of a search, where the changes in search result rankings over time were studied: "When analyzing the fluctuations of results over time and correlating changes with known algorithm updates one can extrapolate the consequences of algorithmic changes to a search engine result page for a particular query" (Weltevrede, 2016, p. 117; see also Rogers, 2013, pp. 91–93, for this example).

However, to provide the source material for this approach, the searches must have been made in the past. Other source types, including patents, are also used to study algorithm changes and their effect on personalization and localization, as well as real-time updates (Weltevrede, 2016, pp. 118–129).

Since "the web as a whole" is not available as such, and therefore not archived as such, a variety of indirect source types that nevertheless originate in the web have to be used, as illustrated by these three examples. Browsers may be studied by the use of screenshots showing web content and incidentally also showing the browser, global web hyperlink networks may be examined through search engine databases, and the visible web in the form of search results may be studied as a proxy to unlock the hidden web of search algorithms. In all cases, the sources had to be collected and preserved in the past—for example, as part of earlier research projects. However, the archived web in web archives may still be useful. For instance, historical knowledge about the hidden side of browsers could be studied by querying web archives' source code for information about which browsers web pages were optimized to be interpreted by.

4.6 Multiple-Strata Cases

Some web history studies examine multiple web strata at the same time, as the following examples show. Each case illustrates general issues relevant to web historiography—history with as well as history of the web—in its own way, and does this by focusing on the visible and the hidden web, including software that tracks web users' behavior.

In the article "A Brief History of Facebook as a Media Text: The Development of an Empty Structure" (Brügger, 2015), the historical development of the semiotic and interactional elements of Facebook, from 2004 to 2013, is studied. Thus, this focuses on two web strata: web elements and website. The article is a follow-up to a smaller study made five years earlier, published in 2009, and at the time the previous study was conducted, versions of Facebook's website were available in the Internet Archive (as thefacebook.com and facebook.com). Initially, the 2015 study was also to have been based on material from the Internet Archive, but apparently the material was no longer available, probably because the website owner had asked that a robots.txt message, indicating that the material was not to be archived, be respected. Thus, the examination of Facebook from 2004 to 2013 had to build on other sources, and given the focus on the visible side of web elements, and their changes over time, screenshots were an acceptable solution. However, although large numbers of screenshots of old Facebook pages were available on the World "Wild" Web, the challenge of dating these sources had to be met by including other source types, such as official press releases and Facebook's blog, with a view to establishing a timeline against which to evaluate the date of the screenshots. Moreover, a year after the article was published, archived versions of Facebook were again available in the Internet Archive, but at the time of writing the present book, the following was found when searching for facebook.com: "Page cannot be displayed due to robots.txt."

This last case illustrates that in web archives that respect the robots.txt, what is actually archived may come and go, as the website owner asks for the web material to be blocked. Also, the project shows that screenshots found on the World "Wild" Web may be used as a historical source for web history, and that the challenges of dating this type of material may be addressed in a satisfactory manner if combined with other sources.

Another example of a study that spans several web strata is Jules Mataly's 2013 master's thesis, *The Three Truths of Margaret Thatcher: Creating and Analysing Archival Artefacts* (Mataly, 2013). This example of history with the web investigates how "the technology of the archive will have impacts on the archived, and therefore also on our interpretation of the archived" (Mataly, 2013, p. 3). The concrete case presented is the web legacy of Margaret Thatcher: "What in ten, twenty years and later will web users, journalists or historians find about Margaret Thatcher on the various web archives?" (Mataly, 2013, p. 28). He investigates this question by looking at differences when the same data is searched for "margaret thatcher" over a seven-year period (2004–2010) in three different collections: the UK Web Archive's special collections, a search on google.co.uk, and the Internet Archive's data set of the .uk web domain (the "JISC UK Web Domain Dataset (1996–2013)"), made searchable through a prototype of a search interface provided by the UK Web Archive (Mataly, 2013, pp. 41–42). In all steps of the data retrieval, digital tools were used.

By exploring how the differences in web archiving may impact research, Mataly's study emphasizes the need to consult different web collections.

In the book chapter "The Case of Web Browser Cookies: Enabling/Disabling Convenience and Relevance on the Web" (Elmer, 2002), Greg Elmer studies the development of web browsers' user interfaces with regard to where information about the browser's use of cookies is located (Elmer, 2002, pp. 50–51). Thus, two web strata are in focus, web elements and the web as a whole, and the invisible elements, cookies, are "seen" as through the textuality of the browser's interface, by focusing on textual web elements such as pulldown menus, boxes, circles, buttons, and written text. This study examines different versions of the Netscape browser (versions 1.12–6.01, from 1995 to 2001), and it debates the pros and cons of studying

Netscape and Internet Explorer, as well as whether there are differences in platforms and operating systems (Mac/PC) (Elmer, 2002, p. 53). The study does not specify how the users interacted with the browsers, but apparently it was based on online interaction with each browser (Elmer, 2002, p. 53). This investigation is an example of how a hidden web element, the cookie, may be studied by the use of a proxy, the visible web in the form of web browsers. It also shows that if a similar study was to be conducted today, the possible problems related to differences in platform and operating system would probably be even more complicated to address: first, old versions of the browsers had to be available, and second, it would have to be possible to make them run on today's computers (some old web browsers may be simulated via oldweb.today).

Finally, in "Historical Website Ecology: Analyzing Past States of the Web Using Archived Source Code" (Helmond, 2017), Anne Helmond studies the historical changes in the use of web trackers on the front pages of the *New York Times* website between 1996 and 2011, by treating the website as an ecosystem and "by examining the source code in which a website's connections with third parties have become inscribed" (Helmond, 2017, p. 139). The focus is on three web strata examined on the hidden level of the web code: a web element (the code for web trackers) on a web page (the front page of nytimes.com), as seen as embedded in a context, a web sphere (what could be termed the tracker sphere, i.e., the system of trackers). By using the Ghostery software that scans web pages for trackers and matches them against a database of known trackers, Helmond developed the Tracker Tracker tool, which can help detect trackers in large collections of websites (Helmond, 2017, p. 147). With this as a stepping-stone, the study is based on hyperlinks of front pages of nytimes.com retrieved from the Internet Archive, which are then scanned for tracking technologies by using the Tracker Tracker tool (Helmond, 2017, pp. 148–149). This study clearly showcases how the source code in the archived web may be unlocked as a web history source with a view to mapping the interplay among web elements, web pages, and a larger web ecology of code.

4.7   Trends in Web History

As the many different examples of web history—with and of the web— illustrate, web history has been addressed in a great variety of ways. When looking at the examples together, some trends may be observed that, by and large, may also be found in the web history literature from which the cases are drawn.

Both the visible and hidden sides of the web have been the subjects of web history studies over the years, but in the early years of web history the main focus was on the visible web and on smaller corpora, whereas later this was supplemented by studies of the web code and larger corpora. This trend tends to be mirrored in the methods used. When only the visible web was studied, well-known methods prevailed (with a few exceptions), whereas new digital methods had to be developed to unlock the hidden code of the web, and to write web history about large portions of the web.

Although web archives were established in the mid-1990s (see section 6.1), self-archiving was the most widespread way of accessing the old web for study, but as the number of web archives started to grow and more user-friendly forms of access were established, the use of web archives seems to have become the standard. This tendency is emphasized by the continuous development of new forms of access, including complete data sets, which have enabled the emergence of researcher interests where web page–centered research is supplemented with a variety of large-scale projects.

In the very early years of web history research, not much attention was given to the fact that the web changed rapidly and that it should therefore be preserved and referred to in a stable form. Later, the establishment of more and more web archives made it clear that this changeability had an impact on how the online web was archived. But people mainly focused on this as a matter relevant to archiving the web, whereas the temporalities and possible inconsistencies of the archived web as displayed, which will be discussed in sections 7.2 and 8.2, were rarely acknowledged. In recent years a high level of consciousness about the various temporalities of the archived web (to be discussed in sections 7.1, 7.2, and 8.2) has emerged, to the point that this has now become common knowledge, and therefore almost need not be mentioned.

As the field of web history, understood as the history of the web, has matured, and web archives have become more user friendly, web history has also slowly started to become history with the web. It is probably fair to say that scholars who were interested in the web in general, in its online form, were more inclined to grapple with the challenges of the archived web, whereas this challenge was greater for someone who was used to studying handwritten documents or print media. In conjunction with the growing interest on the part of historians—both general historians and specialists in various disciplines—in using the archived web, it has also become more common to include several types of sources in web history studies.

Finally, although close collaborations between web archiving institutions and researcher communities have been there from early in web history, this tends to have become much more widespread in recent years, and it comes in a great variety of forms, from individual researchers asking a web archive for help, to researchers and web archives collaborating on research projects. And collaborations often cover all phases of providing and using the archived web, from researchers being involved in setting up archiving strategies, to being involved in the development of search interfaces and analytical tools.

However, it must be emphasized that the phases of all these trends do not replace one another but constitute overlapping historical layers, where screenshots and analyses of web page content exist alongside large-scale analyses of web code and file types, and where new mixed forms continue to emerge. This also goes for the level of methodological reflection on the use of the web as a historical source, where studies with a low level of awareness about the archived web exist alongside studies that are well embedded in ongoing methodological discussions.

As the examples above illustrate, web history in both senses of the word has grown and matured in recent years, and it has proved to be a very rich field of study, with much unexploited analytical potential. Any fragment of the archived web—a snippet of HTML code, a file type, an associated metadata file—has the potential to become the starting point of a web history. However, to unlock the full potential of the archived web as a source, it is necessary to embed the researcher's use of it in a theoretical and methodological framework that systematically addresses the digitality of the archived web.

5 Archiving the Web

This chapter investigates the origins of the digitality of the archived web, namely, how the online web became the archived web. In short, this chapter investigates the process of archiving the web. The ways artifacts and documents were collected, preserved, and documented in the past have always had an impact on what scholars later had available as possible sources, and on how the material could be made available for research. The establishment of a collection is never neutral; all forms of collection and preservation come with sets of constraints and establish possibilities for their future use. As Lubar notes,

Archives reflect and reinforce the power relationships of the institution that organizes them; they represent not just a technological solution, but also an organizational solution. They document and carry out not only knowledge and technique, but also culture and power. (Lubar, 1999, p. 16)

And this is still true of the archived web.[1] However, the politics of the web archive lie not only in the selection policies, but also in the more intangible politics of the archiving process itself. As I will show, the constraints and possibilities related to the archived web are fundamentally different from those associated with other types of collections, because the process of collecting, preserving, and making the online web available is more complex and opaque than is the case with most other source types. The immediacy and taken-for-granted attributes that, to a certain extent, characterize the preservation of many collections cannot be applied to the archived web in the same way. Knowledge about why, and in particular how, the online web was archived is an important prerequisite for any scholar who wants to understand the research that can and cannot be done with the archived web. It should also be emphasized that although the web is a digital medium, its collection and preservation cannot be understood exhaustively through general and broad reflections on digital preservation or new media conservation, if the specific digitality of the web is not acknowledged (see chapter 2). In the final analysis, efficient scholarly use of the archived web presupposes a detailed understanding of the digitality of the web and its changes when collected, preserved, and made available for researcher purposes.[2]

As I show in what follows, any archiving of the web is a constructed representation of the born-digital online web, hence the characterization of the archived web as the reborn web. And since this representation is based on a number of choices concerning the forms and strategies used to create it, the representation is always biased to some extent.[3]

No matter how the online web is collected, preserved, and made available as the archived web, and later found, selected, and analyzed by a researcher, it is changed to some degree by each of these processes. In this sense, the archived web may be considered a construction that is assembled in several different versions. By the time the archived web reaches the researcher who is going to use it, it has already undergone three processes of construction—when collected, when preserved, and when made available—and yet another construction takes place during the researcher's interaction with the material for a research project. Although all these phases of construction may be separated analytically, as will be done in the following discussion, they are closely interwoven and interdependent, as I will also show.

Although the archived web originates in the online web, it has a digitality of its own, and this digitality has an impact on how researchers can utilize it. Therefore, it is worth taking a closer look at the provenance of the archived web—that is, at how the online web became the archived web (the present chapter). It is also desirable to map where the archived web may be found (chapter 6), to identify what characterizes the digitality of the archived web (chapter 7), and to outline some of the challenges and options for the researcher using the archived web (chapter 8).

This section introduces the most widespread types of web archiving and emphasizes some basic choices the web archiving actor, whether an individual, a group, or an institution, faced in the past when they set out to archive the online web. These choices include some general challenges associated with all archiving forms and strategies, and some that are more specific. The emphasis is on the crawled web, since this is the archiving method used by most major web archives (web crawling is explained in greater detail below), but to complete the picture, other methods of collecting and preserving the web are also included.[4] This is because the perspective of this book is that of the scholar who wants to do web history, and so the question is, what types of source material might this scholar have access to?

To highlight the specific digitality of the archived web, I compare it to digitized collections, since they are also transformations of already existing material, although nondigital, and to the born-digital online web, since the digitality of the online web is what is transformed into the archived web in the archiving process.[5]

5.1   Why Archive the Web?

Before discussing in greater detail how the web of the past may be saved, it is worth asking a simple question: Why? Why bother to archive the online web, since it is a born-digital medium already out there, online and searchable? Or, as Viktor Mayer-Schönberger notes in *Delete: The Virtue of Forgetting in the Digital Age*, "The human demand for more comprehensive digital memory will continue to rise. The result is a world that is set to remember, and that has little if any incentive to forget" (Mayer-Schönberger, 2009, p. 91).

However, today's web users may have a different experience. The web has an endless amount of content, but at the same time, a common experience is that what was on the web yesterday or a year ago is no longer there. It may have been moved, changed, or deleted, as illustrated by the changes to the White House website mentioned at the beginning of this book. The web may not forget, but it is also constantly evolving, in most cases without leaving any traces.

The lifetime of web content has been debated since at least the late 1990s. The first studies mainly mapped the changeability of web pages with the aim of improving the web crawling process on which web search engines were built, and these studies are primarily based on experimental web collections, where a certain portion of the web is continuously crawled for the purpose of the study. Cho and Garcia-Molina (1999) concluded that "it takes about 50 days for 50% of the web to change or to be replaced by new pages" (Cho & Garcia-Molina, 1999, p. 7). But they found that there are major variations, depending on the top-level domain, since it took only eleven days for 50% of the .com domain to change, but four months for the .gov domain. In a 2004 study, Ntoulas et al. found that

after almost a year (week 51) nearly 60% of the pages were new and only slightly more than 40% from the initial set was still available. It took about nine months (week 39) for half of the pages to be replaced by new ones (i.e., half life of 9 months). (Ntoulas et al., 2004, p. 4)

Another alternative to studying experimental web collections is to use an already established web collection and to compare this with the online web, with the aim of finding out how much of what was archived is still online. In a 2014 study of the life span of web pages, Agata et al. examined how many of 10 million web pages archived in 2001 were still online: "The survival survey revealed that more than 90% of the web pages had disappeared in the last 12 years. The life span study found that the average life span of a web page is 1,132.1 days" (Agata et al., 2014, p. 464). And in 2015, Jackson compared material archived by the UK Web Archive in 2004–2014 to the online web and showed that "50% of resources [are] unrecognisable or gone after 1 year, 60% after 2 years, 65% after 3 years" (Jackson, 2015, p. 20).

Finally, one could also study the development of domain names as a proxy for how much the web changes. Based on material in the national Danish web archive Netarkivet, the development of domain names on the Danish ccTLD .dk is investigated by Brügger et al. (2017). When archiving the entire Danish web domain Netarkivet starts with the domain names on the authoritative domain name list from dk-hostmaster, the handler of the ccTLD. In the study the domain names on this list were compared to the .dk domain names actually archived during the months the archiving took place, as well as to what could be found of .dk domains from the same period in the Internet Archive. The study showed that web domains come and go with a very high frequency (Brügger et al., 2017, pp. 72–76).

Despite the differences in how changes to the web may be measured and in the estimated lifetime of web content, there seems to be agreement that large portions of the web are very ephemeral. Apparently, although there may be little if any incentive to lose digital memory, the web tends to forget all by itself. Thus, the scholar who sets out to write web history based on web material from the past has to rely on someone having taken the initiative to collect and preserve the web and to make it available for research purposes. If this has not happened, the material is likely to have disappeared.

It is worth noting that the volatile nature of the online web is different from what is known in relation to most digitized collections, mainly because these collections are based on the existence of a stable, nondigital original that may even still exist. Although some types of originals may also be threatened by disappearance, such as newspapers printed on acidic paper that will eventually dissolve, or film that may ignite spontaneously, the life span of this printed material or film is much longer than that of the online web. Also, the threats to acidic paper or combustible film are well described and systematic, in that when these materials were in use most copies were affected, just as their "disappearance" is taking place within the collection, not before the collection was established.

5.2   Is Web Archiving Archiving?

Since the mid-1990s, the term *web archive* has been used to describe any collection of the online web, and consequently, *web archiving* has been used to describe the act of collecting and preserving the online web and making it available. However, it is worth reflecting on the accuracy of this terminology, by questioning the extent to which a web archive is, in fact, an archive.

Cultural heritage institutions are often divided into two types, depending on the kinds of material they collect: those that deal with artifacts, and those that deal with documents, in the broadest sense of the word, including written and printed texts, audio, and video. In the first group one finds museums, and the latter includes libraries and archives. For libraries and archives, another distinction often exists, dependent on the provenance of the collected material. Libraries collect what has been made public, such as books, newspapers, radio, and television, whereas archives collect what has not been made publicly available, like people's diaries, photographs or correspondence, or minutes of meetings and other company documents. (Things are not always as clear as this distinction indicates; overlaps and a variety of exceptions exist.)

Worldwide, the vast majority of web archives hold the publicly available web, whereas collections of the private web are rare (they may include personal email correspondence, companies' intranets, personal profiles on social media, and the like). Despite this fact, the term *web archive* is generally used for both groups of collections, although the collections in the first group are not archives, strictly speaking. If the terminology is to be consistent with the commonly used distinction between libraries and archives, what is now called a web archive should be called a *webrary*. Just as a library is a collection of books (*liber* in Latin), a *webrary* is a collection of web publications, and the term *web archive* should be used only for collections holding the nonpublic parts of the web. But *webrary* is not a good term in itself, because it is not easily pronounced. It also does not work well if used to describe the act of collecting (however, the terms *webliography* and *webography* exist to indicate lists of websites, like a *bibliography* for books; cf. Craven, 2002). Moreover, *web archiving* and *web archive* were coined decades ago, they have been used widely since then, and they are even parts of the names of a number of national and transnational web collections, such as the Portuguese Web Archive, the UK Web Archive, and the Internet Archive. For these reasons, this somewhat confusing and misleading terminology probably has to be accepted, and so *web archiving* is used in this book to indicate the broad activity of collecting and preserving the online web and making it available, regardless of which part of the web is in question (public or private), and *web archive* is used for the results of this activity. But it is important to have this terminological clarification in mind, particularly if scholars expect web archives to be archives in the traditional sense of the word.

5.3   Web Archiving—Forms and Strategies

As mentioned previously, no archiving is neutral; it is always biased, and this also goes for the constructed holdings of web archives. What is important from a researcher's perspective is to have the right tools in place to describe how these biases unfold and how their impact on the research process may be evaluated. In the case of web archives, it is important to look at the forms of archiving used and the strategies adopted. How did the archiving take place, and what were its aims? Although it is important to keep this constructive element in mind, it is equally important to remind ourselves that web archives are not constructed from nothing; in some way they are always based on what was actually online. The challenge is to determine what this way was.[6]

5.3.1 Deliberate and Purposive Collection and Preservation of
Web Material

In the past, the online web may have been archived in various ways. The most widespread archiving form is web crawling, which is used by most major national and international web archiving initiatives, but it is also possible to collect and preserve the web in other ways. Since researchers doing web history may have to combine different forms of the archived web from different collections, a broad understanding of web archiving is desirable. Thus, web archiving is understood as any form of deliberate and purposive collection and preservation of web material. A closer look at each of the elements of this definition highlights what this covers.

Web archiving must include both collection and preservation. This means that the simple act of entering a web address in a web browser's location bar and retrieving an HTML file to be displayed in the browser is not web archiving; although the web material is collected, it is collection without preservation (the computer's cache is not considered preservation). The opposite also holds true: when an HTML file is put on a web server, it is preserved until someone deletes it or the web server closes down. But it is deposited, not collected, so that we have a case of preservation without collection.

Web archiving is deliberate and purposive—that is, the act of archiving must be accompanied by some sort of awareness that one is actually archiving the web. This entails reflection on the motivation for the archiving process, ranging from an immediate and rudimentary sense of the need to preserve what is encountered on the web, to more clearly formulated strategies.

To better understand the purposive element of web archiving, one may distinguish between two general approaches to web archiving: macro and micro web archiving (see Brügger 2005, pp. 10–11). The purpose of macro web archiving is to continuously collect large portions of the web, such as a national web domain (in part or in total), or as much of the global web as possible, often with the goal of preserving the cultural heritage. This form of web archiving is performed by large national or international institutions or companies (including national libraries) with professional knowledge about managing the archiving process, and with large computer setups. The aim of micro archiving is to collect small amounts of web material for a limited period of time, from one single web page to the constituents of a web sphere. This may be done to preserve an object of study, if performed by a (group of) scholar(s), or to document some other web activity, if performed by a journalist or anyone else who wants to keep a record of the web. Micro web archiving is performed by actors with limited technical knowledge about archiving the web and with limited computer power and storage capacity.

In the past, when someone wanted to archive the online web—be it through macro or micro web archiving—the way the collection and preservation were executed had to be considered. Although these considerations may not have always been conscious, they always included at least two elements: the forms of archiving to be used, and the strategy to be adopted during the archiving, to preserve as much as possible of what was intended.

5.3.2   Forms of Web Archiving

Seven forms of web archiving may be identified: (1) making an image, (2) making a screen movie, (3) downloading individual files, (4) web crawling, (5) collecting web material from a database, made available through an application programming interface (API), (6) collecting the web that has been taken off-line and preserved unchanged, and (7) collecting the web as presented in other media types, such as books, film, and television. The latter cannot really be characterized as web archiving, because no active process is taking place with the specific intent to preserve the web, but it is worth including, because, particularly for the early web, this may be the only source available. Thus, the scholar who wants to do web history can find the archived web in the form of images, movies, individual files, the crawled web, collections made available through an API, the reconstructed web, and the web as depicted in other media types. In the following paragraphs each of these forms will briefly be introduced.[7]

One of the simplest forms of web archiving is preserving web content as a still image. This may be done either by taking a screenshot, or by using software that retrieves the web page (based on a URL) and preserves it as an image or pdf file (a dedicated program or browser add-on) (see Brügger, 2005, pp. 47–49). Despite the simplicity of this form of web archiving, it has been widely used to document academic studies. Although in both cases the result is an image file, in the first case only whatever was present in the visible part of the browser window on the screen is preserved, and this is done independently of any access to the web, whereas in the latter case the entire web page is preserved in full length, as it is retrieved from

the web. Also, screenshots do not preserve hyperlinks, whereas this may be
the case with software that downloads content from the web. In general,
a screenshot is an exact reflection of how the screen looked, whereas what
is rendered in a pdf file may not be an accurate representation because of
the behavior of the software. In terms of settings, these are very simple;
they are usually limited to image resolution, image file format, delay in
start of the archiving, and whether several web pages should be saved in
one file.

The screen movie is an extended version of the web preserved as a still
image. Screen movies are filmed records of what took place on the computer screen, either in part or in its entirety, and they are preserved as
movie files. If the on-screen activity is the moving around on a website,
playing a web-based computer game, or watching streamed video on the
web, the screen movie may be considered a form of web archiving.[8] As with
the screenshot, the screen movie as such is not based on the filming software being in contact with the web server, so there is no direct link between
what was filmed and what was retrieved from the web server; instead, the
movie is a function of the actions of the individual making the movie. The
settings for screen movies are very simple; in addition to those relevant to
screen images, they include whether or not the cursor or sound from the
microphone should be captured.[9]

Another simple form of web archiving is downloading individual files
from the web, one by one, be they entire HTML files, files with extractions
of code, such as hyperlink information only, extracted with dedicated software, or downloads of image, audio, or video files that have been part of
a web page (for instance, embedded). This type of web archiving usually is
performed without any settings having to be made.

The most complex form of web archiving is web crawling.[10] Web crawling is a more sophisticated, systematic, and scalable version of preserving
individual files, because it may be automated, and it scales up for large
amounts of web material, which is also why institutions engaged in macro
archiving usually use web crawling.

Web crawling benefits from all three characteristics of the digitality of
the online web, and it is accomplished by using dedicated software that
works like search engine software: a list of web addresses (URLs) is inserted
into the software, then the software contacts the web servers indicated in
the list of URLs with a request for specific web pages and elements. It then

retrieves and stores the files and continues to the next URL on the list. The result of web crawling is a collection of HTML files and the other files that compose a given web page, either stored as they were retrieved, or aggregated in dedicated archiving file formats, such as ARC or WARC.[11] Also, web crawling usually generates various forms of metadata text. First, this includes text about what the crawling was supposed to do, such as the seed list with the URLs to be archived and text with the definition of the scope of the archiving. Second, it includes text about how the crawling was actually performed, stored in so-called log files or similar (in the Heritrix web crawler used by most large web archives, this is the crawl.log file).

The foregoing very simple web crawling scenario is often extended with a recursive process based on what is being archived, since the crawling software may be configured to continuously check the archived web pages for hyperlinks, then follow these links and archive their link target, and then repeat this iterative process as many times as specified in the scope settings. Compared to the other forms of web archiving, web crawling usually demands a large number of settings, to manage the scope of the archiving.[12] For instance, settings include how many levels from the starting URL the software is allowed to go to follow hyperlinks, whether specific file types should be included/excluded, and whether the crawler should stay within the boundaries of a specific web domain or a top-level domain. Settings also indicate when the archiving process should time out, the maximum number of bytes to be collected, the number of retries, whether cookies should be accepted, and whether the robots.txt should be respected. Because web crawling is based on following hyperlinks, combined with the high number of possible settings, to a certain extent the archiving actor does not know exactly what is archived. The web archiving software, Webrecorder (webrecorder.io), combines elements of web crawling with the basic approach known from screen filming, namely, that the archiving mirrors the actions of the user. Webrecorder sits between the web server and the browser, and instead of following links (as web crawling does), it "follows" the user interaction by recording whatever is loaded from the web server to the web browser upon the actions of the user (the result may be replayed online or downloaded as a WARC file).

The web material of the past may also have been collected from a database structure that is still maintained by the owner of the content and that is made available through a remote API—that is, a set of defined specifications for how data may be requested directly from the provider's server with a view to integrating it in another data structure, like an online web server.[13] This sort of preservation of the web of the past is often used by companies, especially social media outlets, because they continually generate content that may be relevant to reuse in the future. What is available through an API is not the web as it would have appeared in a web browser, but the individual elements making up a web page, such as profile information, images, status updates, and "likes" on social media, as well as information not visible in the web browser—for instance, information about geolocation. In this sense, what was archived through an API was not "the web" in the form of an HTML page, but fragments that could be knit together to form a web page. However, although these fragments may also be retrieved and displayed by an app on a mobile device, it still makes sense to consider the material part of the web, because it could also be viewed as a web page.

Since all the above-mentioned elements are retrieved through an API, some sort of data structure needs to be established to handle the different pieces of information retrieved.[14] Old web material made accessible via an API may be available to future researchers if the owner of the content still preserves it and provides access (a sort of "living web archive"), or because it was previously downloaded and preserved—for example, as part of a research project—and is still available as such. In terms of settings, the data fields to be retrieved and included in the data structure that handles the content must be determined.

Finally, old web material may have been preserved in the same form it had in the past, which is the case if, for instance, the owner of the material has taken it off-line and preserved it unchanged, possibly as a copy of a website in the form of HTML files, or as a dump or backup of a content management system (CMS) preserved on a CD-ROM. In some cases this material may be easily viewed; in other cases it is necessary to reestablish some form of the running environment. Web material preserved by the producer may also include prepublic material, such as design outlines, dummies, and beta versions.

The above-mentioned forms of web archiving are based on some sort of deliberate and purposive collection and preservation having been previously carried out. This is not the case with the next form of web archiving, namely, the old web as presented in other media such as newspapers, magazines, journals, books, and even films, television programs, and commercials and TV spots. Particularly with regard to the early web, print and television may be the only available documentation of this history.

5.3.3   Strategies of Web Archiving

The archiving actor of the past not only chose from a range of different forms of web archiving; choices also had to be made concerning which strategy to use, with a view to archiving as much as possible of what was to be archived. The main reason archiving strategies had to be considered is that none of the archiving forms enables the complete archiving of the web in all its dimensions, exactly as it was on the online web. Therefore, since each of the various archiving forms comes with its advantages and limitations, strategies usually have to be formulated to decide what is to be archived and which omissions are acceptable.

Considerations about which web archiving strategies to employ usually revolve around three variables—space, time, and possible use—and in each case the choices made by the archiving actor may be positioned as points on a continuum. Regarding space, at the one end of a continuum, strategies would be aimed at archiving as much as possible; at the other end, they would be aimed at archiving very specific fractions of the web. Regarding time, the strategy used has to address the question of how often the archiving is to be performed; thus this is a continuum with continuous archiving at one end and archiving only specific, delimited points in time at the other. Finally, regarding possible use, the archiving actor is faced with a continuum with an unknown use scenario at one end versus a well-known and precise use case at the other. Thus, in the past, the strategies used to archive the web were situated at different intersections of a grid with all/fractions, continuous/once, and unknown/known.

To give an example of the foregoing, a national web archive whose mission is to collect and preserve the national cultural heritage on the web (macro archiving) may want to archive an entire national web domain, such as .uk, .fr, or .dk, and to do this once per year. Or the same institution may have decided to archive only a fraction of the national web, but at much shorter intervals—for instance, daily or bimonthly. In both cases, exact knowledge of who is going to use the collection in the future and for what purpose is lacking, but possible use cases are indirectly imagined, since the result of the first strategy enables studies that are not very time sensitive, whereas the opposite is the case with the latter. A research group (micro archiving) may have wanted to archive a complete collection of all websites relevant to a research project about a political election, and to do this monthly, or the group may have wanted to continuously collect only a sample of the relevant websites. In both cases, the use is well known and defined as a specific research project.

Archiving strategies are not always formulated; often, the web is archived with the archiving forms available, and without much reflection on strategy. But in many cases strategies are needed. This is particularly true for web archiving institutions, such as national web archives or web archives at research libraries, or in the case of research projects with a very clear aim. In these cases, very precise strategies are usually formulated—from the general collection level to the detailed scope of specific archiving—and they help evaluate the quality of what was collected.

It is evident that some archiving forms do not go hand in hand with some archiving strategies. For example, if a national web archive intends to archive an entire national web, screen filming is not an option, or if an online computer game or a virtual world such as Second Life (secondlife.com) is to be collected, web crawling is not of much use. Thus, the process of web archiving always involves a trade-off between the available archiving forms and the possible archiving strategies.

5.4   General Challenges When Archiving the Web

With a web archiving toolbox comprising the above-mentioned web archiving forms and strategies, it makes sense to take a closer look at some of the challenges with which the archiving actor struggles when collecting and preserving the online web of the past. What follows is an outline of five general challenges that affect archiving forms and strategies.

The first major challenge encountered when archiving the web is that in many cases no stable original exists to go back to in order to check the quality of what was archived. In contrast to a digitized print newspaper or a radio program on tape, the online web may—or may not—be the same when its quality is checked as when it was archived, given the typical rapid changes affecting the web. Therefore this uncertainty itself means that the online web cannot be considered a stable original. Also, the longer the time span between archiving and quality check, and the larger the web entity to be archived, the greater the uncertainty concerning the stability of what was archived.

The second challenge encountered when archiving the web revolves around the "what" and "how" to archive. Any collection and preservation involve decisions about what is to be included in the collection and what is to be omitted, and how the collection, preservation, and access should take place. The "what" and "how" also apply to web archiving, but compared to most other forms of preservation, including digitization, the inevitable choices of "what" and "how" take place in a much more complex, unsystematic, and opaque environment.

"What" to preserve when archiving the web is the aspect that most resembles other sorts of collection, whereas "how" is where the major differences are. When digitizing a collection of newspapers or radio programs, concerns such as brightness and file compression have to be considered. Although these choices have an impact on the result, the number of choices is small, their possible reach is transparent, and if any other actor proceeded in the same manner, the result would probably be identical. In contrast, in web archiving the combination of the complex digitality of the online web and the multitude of archiving forms and strategies, and their mutual calibration, multiplies the number of possible choices considerably. In particular, with regard to web crawling, the archiving process tends to be opaque, since once the archiving software is let loose on the web, the archiving actor does not know exactly what happens and what goes into the web archive. This is partly because the software follows hyperlinks and partly because of the large number of complicated settings involved, many of which have a far-reaching impact. For instance, as the study of the Italian website unibo.it illustrates, material from that website had been unintentionally archived in several national web archives, probably because hyperlinks from an archived web page pointed to unibo.it (Nanni, 2017; cf. section 4.3). Consequently, as I consider in greater detail in section 7.1, any one archiving actor would not be able to proceed in exactly the same manner as another, and the results would very probably be different if several actors were to archive the same web entity. Therefore, in web crawling, the "what" tends to be obscured by the "how": one may have a clear idea of "what" to archive at the outset, but as a consequence of the multiple options of "how," one would not get what was intended, which could mean getting more than what was intended.

Finally, in relation to the "how" of archiving, it is important to bear in mind that when digitizing a newspaper or a radio program, what could be termed the "archiving unit" and its temporal and spatial extensions are largely givens that are functions of the media materiality and the semiotic characteristics of what is digitized. Print newspapers or analog radio programs come with clearcut and obvious temporal/spatial subdivisions set by the producers of these media. Newspapers are published as individual copies at certain intervals, and radio programs are aired over a specific time span, based on a schedule with clearly marked starting and ending times, which is why most digitized collections of newspapers and radio have the copy and the program as defining units. In contrast, the web is a continuum with no clear time and space delimitations. This means that the archiving actor has to create temporal/spatial subdivisions that fit the archiving forms and strategies, where subdivisions that were not an inherent part of the online web are established, and what was a temporal continuum or a spatial borderland in its online form is arbitrarily sliced up.

A third challenge the archiving actor had to struggle with in the past relates to what may be termed the dynamics of updating (Brügger, 2005, pp. 22–24; cf. also Schneider & Foot, 2004, p. 115). As indicated above, the web changes rapidly, for instance by being updated, but updates are not necessarily predictable and regular. Compared to print or electronic media, they do not follow the temporality of a copy that is published at regular intervals (e.g., daily), or radio and television programs that follow a schedule. It is never clear if, when, and where the web is updated. This means that what was archived at the beginning of an archiving process may have changed as the process progressed: the front page of a website could have changed as the archiving moved further down the website structure, and a web page with a social media feed could have received new feeds only seconds after the archiving started.[15] As there is no stable original to go back to, it is very difficult to find out whether updates have taken place, and to evaluate the reach of the possible updates. If this dynamic of updating were applied to digitized collections, it would be as though page 2 of a newspaper was scanned, and when scanning page 10, page 2 suddenly changed, or as though when halfway through the digitization of a radio program, the beginning had changed. This challenge of the dynamics of updating is a somewhat constitutive uncertainty in web archiving and there are no good solutions for it; if the archiving actor were to start the web archiving process over and over, this would probably just add to the confusion, because the number of instances would grow and rapidly become confusing.

The fourth major challenge the web archiving actor may have encountered in the past is that things may have gone wrong during the archiving process. Even with simple archiving forms, such as screen images made by dedicated software, the software may not have rendered the web page properly (images may be missing, textual elements misplaced, etc.). And with more complex web archiving forms, such as web crawling, the potential for error will have grown considerably. The crawler may have encountered file formats that could not be archived (streaming audio/video, JavaScript, etc.), or encountered other technical challenges originating from the digitality of the online web. Examples might have included crawler traps such as a calendar or web page that continually generated new links; the crawler would have continued to send requests to the web server, not stopping until it eventually reached the set limit (either in time or bytes). And since in most cases a stable original to go back to was lacking, remedying the errors would have been difficult. In contrast, if errors occur when digitizing, they are mostly systematic and recurring, which means that they are more easily rectified, and in any case, an original exists against which the error-prone copy may be checked.

The fifth, and last, major group of challenges for the web archiving actor relates to the archiving strategy selected, and to the nexus between the space and time of a given strategy. With regard to space, the major challenge is that web archiving takes time. Therefore, the closer to "all" the strategy gets, the greater the problem created by the time it takes to perform the archiving, because it is not possible to archive "all" at the same time. But the closer the archiving strategy moves toward "fractions," the smaller the problem. With regard to time, the major challenge is that the closer to "continuous" the strategy gets, the more space presents a problem, because large amounts of the online web cannot be archived on a continuous basis. And the reverse is also the case: the closer to "once," the smaller a problem space is.

Finally, regarding the possible use scenarios concerning what is archived, the less is known about the possible use of the archived web, the more of a challenge it is to select the correct archiving forms and strategies. The more the archiving actor knows about what the archived material is going to be used for, the easier it is to select the appropriate approach to archiving.

In summary, regarding strategies, the greatest challenge is that strategies are strategies, and each supports some instances of the online web being archived while hindering others. This is another way of saying that the web cannot be archived in a 1:1 form in all its dimensions.

5.5   Challenges Presented by Specific Forms of Archiving

In addition to the general concerns that cut across web archiving forms and strategies, the archiving actor has had to face some challenges specific to how the different archiving forms handle the archiving of the three relatively fixed features of the online web's digitality: its two textual layers, its fragments, and its hyperlinked nature.

One of the major, distinctive features related to the different archiving forms is whether both layers of the online web are archived, or only one. On the one hand, archiving in the form of an image or a screen movie preserves only whatever was visible on the computer screen or in the browser window, whereas the HTML code is not archived. In this case, what you see is what you get. On the other hand, web crawling (or the preservation of individual files one by one) preserves only the HTML code and the files or services that may be embedded (images, graphics, a feed, etc.), and archiving via API also preserves only the elements as parts of the hidden text. Thus, what is preserved with web crawling and API is not what the users of the past saw in their browsers, but the HTML code that was found on the web server in an HTML file, and in files that were linked to and that were eventually interpreted in the user's browser to form the displayed web page.

There is an imbalance between the two foregoing clusters of archiving forms, because the HTML code cannot be restored from the screen image and screen movie. But what was visible in the past when the HTML code was interpreted in a browser may be restored, although restoring an exact copy is not necessarily easy (see section 7.2 about the Wayback Machine).

The archiving actor faced the challenge of either preserving a given web entity exactly as it looked while excluding the HTML code for good, or preserving the HTML code and other elements, which had to be patched together at a later stage to get as close as possible to what was once actually online.

When making a screen image or movie, the archiving actor may decide to archive only fragments of a larger entity—for instance, only an image or a video stream on a web page, or only one page of a website. In contrast to what takes place with web crawling and API, these fragments are created solely by the archiving actor, independently of what happens on the web server, and they reflect only the visible layer. Thus, either the archived web was archived as fragments created by the archiving actor independently of the online web, or it was archived in the fragmented form it already had on the online web—that is, the HTML files and other files sitting on a web server. Consequently, the archiving actor has had to balance two challenges. In the first case, although she has exactly the fragments she wants, the fragments do not come in a marked-up and uniform form, and therefore it may be difficult to piece together a great variety of such fragments. In the latter case, she may not have the precise fragments needed, but the fragments come in an already marked-up and machine-readable form, either in the HTML code, in the file extension, or as part of a database (API), which may make it easier to interact with the material in the research process.

Finally, active hyperlinks are usually not archived when the web is archived by the use of screen images or movies (see section 5.3); in some cases they may be (if software dedicated to do this is used), but the hyperlinks then point to the online web and not to an archived web entity. In contrast, web crawling is based on following hyperlinks, and hyperlinks are usually also included in databases accessible via API, which is why hyperlinks are normally archived with these forms.

The foregoing differences mean that the challenge the archiving actor faces is whether exact renderings of what was online are needed, at the expense of not having access to hyperlinks, or whether hyperlinks should be preserved, knowing that this may entail challenges when delimiting what is archived and when handling temporal and spatial inconsistencies in replaying the archived material at a later stage (see section 7.1).

6 The Web of the Past—Where to Find What?

A first step for the scholar who wants to use the web of the past as a source for writing web history—either as history with the web or history of the web—is to find preserved versions of yesterday's web. During the last two decades, vast amounts of the web have been collected and preserved, but nevertheless, it is likely that when searching for the old web, either no material or only partly relevant material is available. But the preserved web may be found in a variety of places, and it has usually been collected and preserved with different aims, by different actors, and with different degrees of access, and therefore having different arrays of possible use.

Today there are a great number of web archiving initiatives, and it is not possible to introduce each existing web collection. Instead, this chapter gives an overview of the major types of collections of the web of the past by highlighting their aims, legal frameworks for collecting and providing access, and archiving forms and strategies used. I also discuss the forms of access and the knowledge required to use different types of collections and the levels of documentation involved.[1]

This overview presents only collections, and not the archiving services offered by professional or commercial vendors. The latter cannot be considered collections in their own right for the most part. Instead they function as subcontractors, archiving the web for some of the collection holders mentioned below, such as web archives, research groups, universities, museums, and companies. These vendors usually use web crawling and include the Internet Archive's subscription service, Archive-It, as well as the Internet Memory Research's Archivethe.Net.[2]

Finally, it is worth mentioning that each web collection comes with a history of its own. As the following paragraphs demonstrate, collections often change their archiving procedures (forms, strategies, technical solutions), legal frameworks may be altered, and new forms of access may be provided. Therefore, it is important for researchers searching for the old web to also take the historical development of each collection into consideration. Unfortunately, web archives rarely document and communicate their own history in a manner that is useful to researchers.[3]

6.1 Transnational Web Archives

For anyone who wants to study the archived web, the most important sources are probably the institutions committed to preserving the web, either on a transnational scale—as is the case with the Internet Archive, which, in principle, archives the entire web—or as defined by geography, such as a nation, state, region, or city.[4]

The largest collection of this type (or of any type) is the Internet Archive (archive.org), founded in 1996 by American internet entrepreneur Brewster Kahle. The Internet Archive is a nonprofit organization, based in San Francisco, with the aim of preserving digital media, including the web. The Internet Archive started by establishing a collection of the websites of the 1996 American presidential candidates (see Kimpton & Ubois, 2006, p. 202), but soon after it launched its broad web collections based on web crawling.

The Internet Archive is not limited to collecting the web related to a specific geographic area (a nation or part of a nation), but instead collects material to which hyperlinks point, which means that in principle, any web entity to which a link points has been archived (for a detailed history of the Internet Archive, see Kimpton & Ubois, 2006; Webster, 2017b). Thus, the strategy of the Internet Archive is to archive as much as possible. In addition to the web archiving initiated by the Internet Archive itself, it is also possible to submit an individual web page to have it archived, or to deliver old web material to the archive. It is also worth noting that the Internet Archive (in general) respects a website owner's wish to not have the website crawled, as expressed by the robots.txt file, and this also applies if a website owner requests that already crawled material be removed. For instance, this happened when sources were collected to support the study of the historical development of the semiotic and interactional elements on Facebook from 2004 to 2013 (Brügger, 2015; cf. section 4.6).

The Internet Archive's collections are freely accessible online via the Wayback Machine, which aims to display the web in a form as close as possible to how it looked when seen through a browser in the past. The web address (URL) of the web page one wants to retrieve is input in the search interface, and if the material is found in the archive, the Wayback Machine presents the web page (also see section 7.2 about the Wayback Machine).[5]

Since early 2017 the Internet Archive has extended its search facilities by providing free text search of all web domain front pages. It is also possible to access the Internet Archive's web collection through a number of different APIs to retrieve information about the archive's content. Finally, the Internet Archive provides researcher access to its Archive-It collections through the Archive-It Research Services (ARS), which allow for the extraction of data such as metadata, link graphs, and named entities from the collections.

Access through the Wayback Machine does not require any special knowledge, whereas access via API and ARS requires some programming skills. The Internet Archive does not provide any detailed documentation about the provenance of the collected web.

In addition to being available through the Internet Archive, the web of the past may be found in the transnational web collection called Common Crawl (commoncrawl.org). The Common Crawl Foundation is a nonprofit organization founded in 2007 by IT entrepreneur Gil Elbaz; its goal is to preserve and provide access to the archived web.

Common Crawl started crawling the web in 2008, and since 2014 one broad crawl is made almost every month. The crawled web is publicly available in an open repository, stored on Amazon Web Services' Public Data Sets. The material may be downloaded for free, or analyzed directly on Amazon's cloud platform. Although access is free, the material is not presented in any browsable form; it has to be downloaded as an entire corpus for each crawl, and some programming skills are needed to access the material. There is very little documentation about the archiving process, but metadata information is included in the downloadable data sets.

6.2   National, Regional, and Local Web Archives

In parallel with the establishment of the Internet Archive, a number of national web archiving initiatives were launched. In most cases, these collections were established and hosted by already existing organizations, each with its specific remits and collection policies that were mainly reapplied to the web. For instance, web archives established by national libraries archive what was published within the boundaries of a nation or is of interest to its citizens, whereas national and government archives preserve the nation's unpublished web record or government information published on the web. A national institution that preserves the nation's audiovisual cultural heritage collects the web related to radio and television (as is the case with the French web archive at the Institut National de l'Audiovisuel (INA)), and a national institution that provides computer services to academic and scientific communities preserves public content in computer networks of national interest (as is the case with the Portuguese Web Archive).

One of the first national web archiving initiatives was PANDORA: Australia's Web Archive in 1996, and in the years since, a large number of national web archives have been established. The main aim of these web archives is to collect and preserve the web material that is somewhat linked to the nation in question, but how this is determined varies. In some cases, this includes web material on the country's national top-level domain (as a whole or in part), and it may be supplemented by a number of other criteria (website owner living in the country, content about the country, etc.). In other cases, specific subdomains are targeted where such exist, such as the United Kingdom's .gov.uk.

A nation need not be the unifying geographic entity for a web archive. There are also web archives aimed at archiving the web within the limits of a continent, such as the project known as the Current Events in Africa Web Archive (CEAWA) (hosted by the Internet Archive's subscription service Archive-It), or within the boundaries of a region (e.g., PADICAT, the Web Archive of Catalonia), or a city (e.g., Antwerp City Archives in Belgium).

With regard to the legal framework that underpins web archiving, some collections are based on a legal deposit law, whereby the web archive is permitted to collect and preserve all web material (such as the UK Web Archive and the national French or Danish web archives). In other countries, collection is based on an opt-out approach, where website owners are notified that their web content will be archived, and if they do not object, this is considered implicit permission (this is the case with the Dutch web archive). Differences also exist with regard to whether the desire to not have one's website crawled (as expressed by a robots.txt file) is respected. For instance, the Portuguese Web Archive does respect robots.txt, whereas the legal deposit law in Denmark entitles the Danish Netarkivet to ignore this.

The most widespread form of web archiving is web crawling, but in some cases this is supplemented by other forms. For example, since 2014 the UK Web Archive has also taken screenshots of the front page of each crawled website, the Danish Netarkivet has archived examples of Second Life by screen filming (available at netarkivet.dk/netarkivet-arkiverer-second-life), and the French web archive at the INA also archives via API.

The national web archives vary significantly in terms of archiving strategies, from broad collections aimed at archiving as much as possible of a national web domain without much curatorial involvement (e.g., the UK Web Archive and the Danish Netarkivet archive entire national web domains), to collections of carefully selected websites (such as the Australian PANDORA). However, most national web archives adopt a combination of several strategies, thus combining broad national web crawls with thematic collections of specific sections of the national webs related to events, topics, or similar demarcations.

Regarding access to web archive collections, the terms of accessibility vary, mainly because different national legal frameworks apply. In some countries, national web archives are online and available to all (e.g., the Library of Congress, the Portuguese Web Archive, and the Icelandic Web Archive), whereas in other cases, access is restricted to various degrees, from being available to everyone but with onsite access only (the UK Web Archive's Legal Deposit collection, or the Dutch Web Archive), to being accessible to researchers only but with online access (such as the Danish Netarkivet), and to the Norwegian web archive, Web Archive Norway, which offers no access at all.

Access to national web archives is available mostly via the Wayback Machine or similar, but full text search may also be available, as is the case with the Australian PANDORA, the Portuguese Web Archive, and the Danish Netarkivet. In addition to providing access through the Wayback software and free text search, some national web archives, such as the Portuguese Web Archive, now offer access via API, and in some cases derived data sets may be available—for instance, in the "JISC UK Web Domain Dataset (1996–2013)" (see section 4.3.1).

At present, the form and amount of documentation provided by (trans) national web archive collections range from curated metadata about individual websites (as seen in the Library of Congress web archive), to very general documentation on a collection level, or almost no documentation.

As previously mentioned, legal frameworks, archiving forms, and strategies change over time. For instance, the UK Web Archive started in 2005 by collecting only British institutions' websites, based on their historical, social, and cultural significance, but after a new legal deposit law was passed in April 2013, the archive has also been allowed to archive the whole of the UK web domain. Other examples are the Danish Netarkivet, which has created opportunities for special archiving suggested by researchers, and the above-mentioned case of the French INA, which has started archiving via API, which was not initially done.

6.3   University Libraries, Museums, and Researchers

Although transnational and national web archives hold large collections of the archived web, they are not the only institutions where one may look for the web of the past. Web collections have also been established at many university libraries, often to support faculty research interests or to expand an already established preweb collection, such as the UCLA Library's UCLA Online Campaign Literature Archive, aimed at documenting local election campaigns (archive-it.org/collections/5903).

Some museums and arts communities have established web archives to ensure the preservation of works of art that are created and made available on the web only.[6] An example of this is ArtBase, established by the Rhizome arts organization in 1998, which holds over 2,000 pieces of internet art, including websites (rhizome.org/art). Another type of museum with archived web holdings is the self-described "web museum"—that is, a museum of the web of the past, such as the Web Design Museum, which curates an exhibition of web design trends between 1996 and 2005 (webdesignmuseum.org), or the Danish Webmuseum.dk (webmuseum. dk). Finally, the oldweb.today initiative is an online service where the display of the old web archived in publicly available web archives is emulated in old web browsers, including Mosaic, from the early 1990s. The above-mentioned types of web collections are usually freely accessible to the public online and are often well documented.

Web material from the past may also have been archived by research groups or individual scholars as part of a research project. This type of material often takes the form of micro archiving, but the use of professional vendors such as Archive-It is also widespread. In some cases, researcher-generated collections are publicly available, such as The Human Rights Web Archive @ Columbia University, which was established as a collaboration between researchers and a university library (hrwa.cul.columbia .edu).

As the foregoing collections were established to facilitate specific research projects, in many cases they may not be publicly available, just as it may be difficult to even find this type of old web material in any systematic way, because usually no overview of such collections exists. They may have been deposited in local, national, or transnational research data storage services (such as Academic Torrents in the United States (academictorrents.com) or the European Zenodo (zenodo.org)), with restricted access, but currently there is very little precedent for researchers studying the web to deposit their collections. Thus, the old web collected by research groups or individual researchers usually has to be identified in more unsystematic and haphazard ways, by querying relevant researcher networks, checking research publications, and the like. However, one should bear in mind that since this type of material was archived to support a specific research project, it may be customized to such an extent that it is not usable in other studies. When it comes to archiving forms and strategies, all those mentioned in section 5.3 may have been used, depending on the research question the collection was established to help investigate. Since this sort of material was collected specifically for research purposes, it is usually well documented.

6.4 Activist Web Collections

In contrast to the above-mentioned collections that originate in formal institutions with an obligation or need to preserve the web of the past, more loosely organized grassroots organizations have emerged, uniting individuals or groups who wish to preserve the web. Although these web archiving projects share with the official actors a fundamental commitment to preserving the web, their approach is much more activist and ad hoc, often spurred by the fact that specific parts of the web are threatened with removal or deletion, and therefore should be collected here and now. One of the most prominent web collections of this type is the Archive Team's Geocities Snapshot, which is a preserved copy of GeoCities, a web service established in 1994, where users could create their own web presence. GeoCities was bought by Yahoo! in 1999 and closed down in 2009, but before that happened, the Archive Team had started to archive the website (available at archiveteam.org/index.php?title=GeoCities). The Archive Team (archiveteam.org) was established in 2009 with the aim of preserving parts of the web in danger of being lost, often web services holding valuable personal or shared content. The Archive Team's Geocities Snapshot is examined, for example, by Milligan (2017; cf. section 4.3).

Many of the Archive Team's collections are hosted by the Internet Archive, where they are available for browsing via the Wayback Machine, and are freely downloadable as data sets. If the collections are downloaded as entire data sets, some programming skills are needed to interact with the material. The documentation of the content of the collections is not strong.

6.5   Social Media Databases

As previously mentioned, in the past, one way of archiving the web was by retrieving web material from a database via an API—for instance, as seen with social media such as Facebook and Twitter. But insofar as the content to which the API gives access is still available, the content of such databases may itself constitute a collection of old web material. However, it is important to keep in mind that these collections were not made to preserve the web material for future researcher use, but to support the social media company's business model, including user profiling and tailoring advertisements to users. Retrieving this type of historical material is possible only if the social media company still provides access to it, either directly to researchers, or to a retail data outlet with extended access from which the researchers may then purchase the data.

Since the aim of the social media company's API is not to preserve a historical record that is as accurate as possible, and since there is no way of finding out the extent to which the social media company or the data vendor actually provides what is requested, it is very difficult to evaluate how comprehensive the material is. In many cases, only randomly generated samples are provided, without information about the samples, just as specific types of data may have been censored out, deleted by the user, or just discarded since the material was originally created. The technical setup of the API may also change, giving different results depending on when the database is accessed (cf. Lomborg and Bechmann, 2014, p. 260; Kumar et al., 2015, pp. 40–41). Since documentation about what has been preserved (and what has not) is almost always lacking, it may be difficult to determine what is in a collection. However, these challenges may be partly overcome if researchers can base their investigations on already created collections of clearly identified material that may later be collected via an API. For instance, this is possible via catalog services such as "Tweet ID Datasets" (www.docnow.io/catalog), where one may find data sets of Tweet identifiers that have been previously uploaded (but not the Tweets themselves). These identifiers may then be used to extract the desired Tweets or to establish which Tweets are missing from an extraction.

As previously mentioned, material from an API comes in the form of the individual elements a web page may consist of, which is why some sort of data structure is necessary to handle the different pieces of information. Thus, material retrieved via API does not look like web pages in a browser but is instead a table with rows and columns, each with bits of information. If one retrieves the raw data oneself, some skills are needed to handle the information. If a vendor is used, a data structure is often provided for viewing and analyzing the material, but research is then limited to the forms offered for viewing and analysis.

6.6   Restored Collections

The web that had actually disappeared from the online web in the past may still be found online, but in a restored form. This occurs when web enthusiasts with an interest in a specific website (or similar) have dug up web material that was taken off-line at some point but kept in its original form. They have then meticulously reestablished the website in the original form or as close to this as possible. This has happened with material from the earliest web server, info.cern.ch, which has been restored and put online (see first-website.web.cern.ch; see also Koerbin, 2017), as well as with the first website outside Europe, the website of the SLAC National Accelerator Laboratory at Stanford University. The latter website may be found in a restored form at the Stanford Web Archive Portal (see swap.stanford.edu; cf. Karampelas, 2014).[7]

The aim of web restoration projects is somewhat similar to that of activist grassroots programs, namely, to make the vanished web available to a wider public. The difference is that collections of the restored web are not based on archiving the web before it disappeared, but on reconstructing the already vanished web. This type of old web is mainly accessible online, and since the people or institutions that have recreated the website have invested a lot of time and effort in acquainting themselves with the old web material, these websites are usually also very well documented.

6.7 The World "Wild" Web

Although the online web may not be considered a collection in the strict sense of the word, it may very well be a treasure trove of old web material. The uncurated World "Wild" Web may have two main types of old web material: on the one hand, screenshots—or even screen movies—of old web pages that someone made in the past and put online for whatever reason, and on the other hand, old web material that was put online in the past and is still there, unchanged, either because the owner wanted it to remain there or because its existence was forgotten. Examples of the first type are early screenshots of browser windows on Tim Berners-Lee's desktop (cf. www.w3.org/MarkUp/tims_editor), screenshots of old Facebook pages, or screen movies of social media such as MySpace. An example of the latter type is the website "Design Patterns for Avionics Control Systems," which, in 2002, was used as an example of early web page design by Engholm (2002, p. 199). As of 2017 it is still located at the original web address, http://g.oswego.edu/dl/acs/acs/acs.html, where it went up in 1995—apparently unchanged, still with a "Last revised" date of 1995 (other examples can be found in Nagy, 2012). A subtype of the latter is the blog, since they are often de facto collections of the old web, because of their preservation of old blog posts in reverse chronological order (however, it is never clear whether the website layout has changed).

Since material found on the uncurated World "Wild" Web was just left behind online and is not embedded in any curatorial practices, usually there is no systematic way of finding it, except for searching the web for the relevant topic, and limiting the search to "images" or "video," which may provide very useful material. However, particularly with screenshots/screen movies, it may be challenging to determine the provenance of the material, including its date. Since this type of old web material is "preserved" online, it also presents the same challenges as the rest of the online web, namely, that it is volatile, changed, or (re)moved. Examples include the website with the Mosaic browser's original documents from 1993, and the "What's New" web page on the NCSA website from 1993 to 1996, both of which were still online in 2005, unchanged, when I drafted the monograph *Archiving Websites: General Considerations and Strategies* (see my reference to these web pages in Brügger, 2005, p. 15). But none of them are still retrievable at the original addresses; they may be found only in the Internet Archive.

Finally, although old web material is still online, the technical environment for displaying it and making it function properly may no longer be available.

6.8 Nondigital Formats in Other Media Types

As mentioned in section 5.3, copies of the web of the past may have been preserved in nondigital formats in other media types, particularly in print media such as newspapers, magazines, or books about the web and its use (like Krol, 1992), or in academic journals with analyses of the web. The old web may even be found in television programs. For instance, a very early version of the White House website was part of one of the first news items about the internet on Danish television, on December 11, 1994, and included the voice of President Bill Clinton, welcoming visitors to the website. (Whitehouse.gov is not available in the Internet Archive until 1996, but the November 1995 version may be found in the National Archives, without the president's welcome message but with that of the vice president. It is available at clintonwhitehouse1.archives.gov.) Commercials and TV spots for websites and services are also valuable source records of the old web.

Particularly when studying the early web, print and electronic media may be the only available sources. Obviously, these instances of the old web were not made with a view to preserving the web, which makes it difficult to find them in any systematic way, other than in publications that are clearly about the web.

7 The Web of the Past as a Historical Source

The scholar who intends to do web history may have found the old web in one of the above-mentioned types of collections. This reborn web was already constructed once, when the online web's digitality was transformed into the archived web during web archiving. But when the archived material entered the collection, two other forms of construction took place: the process through which it was preserved and the process through which it was made available. Both processes are in part a function of how the web archiving was performed, since the forms and strategies used establish an array of possibilities and constraints concerning how the archived web may be preserved and made available, and later used by a researcher.

This chapter presents some of the main characteristics of the archived web, as a researcher may find it in a web collection, ready to be used as a historical source and interacted with through the research process. First, I identify some constitutive characteristics of the reborn web's digitality; they are considered constitutive in the sense that they cut across the archiving forms and strategies used, because they relate to the transformation of the born web into the reborn web generally. Second, I introduce several specific problems; they are specific insofar as they are a function of how the archived web's digitality is handled in a collection. In particular, which of the two textual layers of the online web was archived—the visible or hidden layer—affects how material may be preserved and made available as part of a collection. Collections where the visible text was fragmented by the archiving actor, and where no hyperlinks were preserved, come with other constraints and possibilities for preservation and availability than collections with the hidden text preserved, such as HTML and adjacent files as well as functioning hyperlinks (see section 7.5). To highlight both the constitutive and the specific characteristics of the archived web, I make comparisons to digitized collections and the online web, where relevant.

7.1 Constitutive Characteristics of the Reborn Web

Independently of archiving forms, strategies, and collections, the archived web has a number of characteristics that are functions of archiving the online web's digitality, and so they may be considered an inherent part of the archived web material. Although not all the points in what follows necessarily apply to all forms or to the same extent, in general the archived web has the following characteristics: an original is lacking, it is incomplete, it is a unique version and not a copy, and there is temporal and spatial inconsistency between the archived fragments. When all these constitutive features of the reborn web are put together, the major overall characteristic is that of a constitutive uncertainty concerning the relation between what was once online and what is found in a collection.

7.1.1 Lack of an Original

One of the major challenges of the web archiving process—that no stable original exists to go back to and check the quality of what was archived—recurs when the archived web is made available in a collection. As previously mentioned, the online web as a whole changes rapidly, and as time goes by, the original that was once online is likely to have disappeared or changed to some degree. Therefore, if things are missing or are not functioning in an instance of the archived web, one cannot expect to go back to the online web and check the original of the version in the collection. The closest one gets to the survival of an original years after a web element appeared online is the case of material retrieved via an API. It may be argued that what is retrieved years later is still the original, but as mentioned above, things may have been deleted or the technical setup of the API may have changed, assembling the bits and pieces differently than was originally the case.

Restored web, such as the cases mentioned in section 6.6, may be based on detailed descriptions of an original. But still, the original is gone, and regardless of the work of the restoration teams, it is a reconstruction based on old bits and pieces.

The only vestiges of the old web that may be considered original years later, at least to some extent, are the copies of the old web found on the World "Wild" Web.

The absence of a stable original is one of the major differences between a digitized collection and the archived web. In many cases, the nondigital original that was once digitized may still exist, and thus it is possible to use this for comparison in cases of doubt.

7.1.2 Incompleteness

Incompleteness is a constitutive element of any kind of collection, either because of deliberate choices concerning what to include or omit, or because various circumstances have affected the collection and preservation processes (fire, water damage, power outages, etc.). However, the incompleteness of the archived web comes in different forms and has different causes than other collections do, including digitized collections.

It may be useful to distinguish between two forms of (in)completeness: on the one hand the completeness of what is to be collected and preserved, before it is archived, and, on the other hand, the completeness of what was preserved, compared to what could have been preserved. Whereas the first relates to the original, the latter is a result of the archiving process. In the case of a digitized collection, what is digitized will be (in)complete if the nondigital original is (in)complete, be it an entire collection or individual copies, and the degree of completeness is usually known from the outset. Concerning the latter type of (in)completeness, to some extent the transformation from nondigital into digital creates an incomplete copy when comparing the nondigital original to the digital version. For example, the transformation of paper-based text into digital writing, the compression of sound, or the making up of page layout with any sort of transcription, may be considered losses. But compared to the incompleteness of the archived web, these shortcomings are systemic and transparent and may be accounted for.

The incompleteness related to the archived web is different from the above, in two respects. First, because an original cannot be found years later, it is impossible to evaluate how complete it was at the time of collection; second, and for the same reason, it is very difficult to evaluate the completeness of the archived web compared to what was once online and what may have been collected.

Although to a large extent the completeness of a digitized collection may be evaluated systematically, as the reasons for possible incompleteness are more transparent, it is very difficult to evaluate the completeness of the archived web with the same systematic approach relative to what was probably online. There are several reasons for this, each of which adds to the opacity. First, the original may be lacking. Moreover, the complexity of the archiving form chosen (its settings and strategies), where it is not always clear what exactly is missing, combined with the fact that choices are rarely documented sufficiently, also make it difficult to reconstruct the choices and to evaluate their consequences for what may be missing. Second, the likelihood of the web being updated during the time it was being archived (the dynamics of updating) may make it difficult to explain why things are missing relative to what could have been collected. Web pages may have been updated or deleted during the archiving of a website, and entire websites on a national top-level domain may have been created or taken down after the archiving of the national domain was started (cf. Brügger et al., 2017, pp. 72–79). Third, something may have gone wrong in the archiving process, owing to technical or human error (or a combination), which poses yet another possible difficulty when evaluating whether something is missing from a collection of the archived web.

Owing to an opaque combination of the chosen archiving strategy, deliberate omissions, updating during the archiving, and archiving errors and insufficiencies, the researcher using a collection from the archived web should expect missing elements, ranging from individual web elements such as images, sound, video, feeds, and forms of interaction, to entire web pages, websites, or large portions of the web.

It is evident that the shorter the time interval of the archiving, the smaller the amount of archived material, and the less complex the web archiving, the greater the chance everything was archived. Therefore, things that have been archived in the form of an individual file or as a screen image tend to be closer to what was once online, whereas large web crawls tend to be less so. But the inherent uncertainty concerning the possible incompleteness of the archived web remains, and therefore the web scholar will probably have to make do with web material that may be expected to be incomplete in various ways and degrees, compared to what was once online. However, what is specific to web archives is not their incompleteness, but that they are incomplete in ways that make it very difficult to determine whether they are incomplete at all, and to explain and account for what is missing, from where, and why. But as will be shown in section 9.2, there are ways of evaluating the possible incompleteness, at least to some degree.

7.1.3   A Unique Version and Not a Copy

Compared to what was once online, the archived web is best characterized as a unique version and not a 1:1 copy. The different choices regarding archiving forms and strategies, combined with the fact that things may be missing (for the reasons mentioned above), means that the same online entity archived in the past by two different archiving actors may prove to be different versions, instead of identical copies of what was online at the time of archiving.[1]

A collection of the archived web is essentially a collection of versions, each of which is a unique construction of an online original that is probably lost. Also, each version is just one version among others, and it is difficult to claim that one of them is an original that is identical to the web material as it looked when online, just as it is challenging to try to reestablish how the online material may have looked, based on the different existing versions (see section 9.2). Therefore, researchers must treat the archived web as a set of unique versions, rather than copies.

The uniqueness of each archived version of the web is different from what usually characterizes a digitized collection, where the result of digitization may be considered a copy that is much closer to being an identical copy of an original.

7.1.4   Temporal and Spatial Inconsistency between
the Archived Fragments

In its online form the many bits and pieces of the web are always present in the same time and space: hyperlink source and target are there at the same time, and a given website has the spatial extension that it has at any given moment. In short, the online web is consistent with regard to time and space. This also goes for missing material at a link target where an error message is received, because the material linked to is no longer there (response code 404). Although the material at the link target is gone, there is consistency between the link source and the error message, and what is important is that the link target does not show something that, in fact, no longer exists or that does not yet exist. Digitized collections mainly appear to be as consistent as the original collection was before being digitized—for instance, in a collection of digitized newspapers, the copies reflect the same chronology as the originals and are there in equal numbers. This is not the case with a collection of the archived web, since it may be inconsistent with regard to time and space, in both cases because the archiving process takes time, and the online web may have changed during that time, thus making the fragments in the archive inconsistent when recombined.

The foregoing possible temporal inconsistency affects all instances of the archived web where hyperlinks are involved, and since the hyperlink is a constitutive element of the online web's digitality (see section 2.2), temporal inconsistency is very widespread in a web archive collection. The temporal coexistence of hyperlink source and hyperlink target on the online web is broken if the link source is archived hours or days before the link target to which it points, which is very often the case. This may affect all web strata—for example, if a web page retrieves and embeds an image, a news feed, or a piece of text from another web server based on a hyperlink, and this fragment was not archived simultaneously with the web page, or if web pages on a website or in a web sphere contain hyperlinks that point to other web entities that were not archived at the same point in time.

The possible lack of temporal coherence between the link source and the link target is not seen in a digitized collection, simply because hyperlinks are optional and may be added after digitization to facilitate navigation; in contrast, the hyperlink is an integral and indispensable part of the online web. If the temporal inconsistency of the archived web was applied to a collection of newspapers it would correspond to an article referring to another article in the following day's newspaper, but once this article is consulted, it is from a copy that was published two weeks earlier or three weeks later.

The possible spatial inconsistency is caused by the fact that all web entities are not necessarily archived with the same spatial extension, which may happen because of deliberate decisions to discard specific parts of the web during the archiving, because of unexpected problems, or because parts of the web were deleted or moved during the archiving process. For instance, in a selection of websites, all websites may not have been archived to the same depth below the front page, thus making this selection spatially inconsistent relative to the websites in their online state. This would be as though in a newspaper collection the size of the newspapers was inconsistent, with some of the copies having only the front page, others having only pages 2 and 4, and yet others having several sections of the paper.

The possibility of temporal and spatial inconsistency affects all web collections, but the longer the time interval and the bigger the entity investigated, the greater the risk of such inconsistencies. Nevertheless, it may be very difficult to evaluate the extent of these inconsistencies. Even the suspicion of possible inconsistency may affect any study based on an analysis of hyperlinks or on the existence of archived web entities of the same size (see sections 8.1 and 8.2).

A collection of the archived web is a collection of bits and pieces from the online web of the past, but it is difficult to establish with certainty the extent to which all the bits and pieces are there, whether they are the right ones from the right points in time, and whether the right ones are linked to each other. The absence of an original to go back to, combined with the uniqueness of each version, endows an archived web collection with a constitutive uncertainty as to the status of the reborn web as a mirror of the online, born-digital web. Also, the scarcity of useful documentation to help provide meaningful answers in cases of doubt makes it even more difficult to navigate these uncertainties.

7.2 Specific Characteristics of the Reborn Web

All instances of the archived web share the general characteristics outlined above to some degree, but each different type of collection may also have specific characteristics of its own that are a function of how the content of the collection was created, how it is preserved, and how it is made available, including how researchers can access and interact with the material.

As mentioned in section 5.5, a fundamental distinction may be made between what portions of the online web are actually collected and preserved. Hence, a web collection may consist either of individual files not directly related to the online web's digitality (if based on screen images or movies), or of bits and pieces originating directly from the online web (if based on downloaded individual files, crawled web, or API). As a consequence, a given web collection may display what was photographed or recorded at the time of archiving—essentially, "What you see is what you can get." Or the collection has to reassemble the archived fragments in a meaningful way to enable their display or otherwise provide access to the collection's holdings, adding yet another layer of construction to what was already constructed during the archiving process. Therefore, as a historical source, the archived web has different characteristics depending on whether it is found in a collection where "What you see is what you can get" or where "What you can get is what may be assembled"—that is, collections based on screen images or screen movie files, as opposed to collections based on web crawling and API, respectively. Each of these types of material, as presented in specific collections, may be considered a subform of the digitality of the archived web, and in both cases some of the constitutive characteristics of the archived web come in specific shapes.

7.2.1 "What You See Is What You Can Get"

Screen images and screen movies are the simplest ways of preserving the web, yet they may be very useful sources for many research projects. They are mainly found in collections in university libraries, in museums (including web museums), in collections made by research groups or individual scholars, and on the World "Wild" Web. The simplicity of this type of archived web is mirrored in the characteristics of the material, and thereby in how it enables researcher interaction. Since screenshots are image files, they do not come with any immediate form of interaction other than allowing the image to be viewed; no moving web elements such as video or animated images are included, hyperlinks are inactive, and it is not possible to see the parts of a web page that were originally outside the image frame.

Individual web pages archived with dedicated software are also still images, and therefore they do not show moving elements, but hyperlinks may work, although only pointing to the online web and not to another still image in a collection. Also, since the web page was archived as such, it is possible to scroll up and down to see the entire web page. Whereas screenshots are not searchable, in many cases web pages archived with dedicated software may be searched, but only within each individual file, not across files.

Since screen movies are movies they unfold over time, and therefore they enable backward or forward movement. But since they do not mirror the structure of the website (or similar) that they depict, but the actions of the individual who initially created the movie, it is only possible to move around in the archived web as filmed. Moving web elements such as videos may be parts of the film, and hyperlinks may have been clicked, but since the screen movie was created independently of the website as such, in both cases these features may be interacted with only as part of the movie, and not as autonomous entities. For the most part, screen movies are not searchable.

7.2.2 "What You Can Get Is What May Be Assembled"

Collections based on archiving and preserving fragments of the web come in two main forms, either as the crawled web, or in the form of material collected via API. But since there are major differences between the two—the first archives what is present on a web server, the latter retrieves content from a database—they are treated separately.

The largest collections of the archived web are based on web crawling, and they include transnational and national web archives, university libraries, museums, some research groups or individual scholars, and publicly available collections created by activists. Thus, these types of collections constitute some of the most important historical sources of web history. The following paragraphs outline some of the general characteristics of the crawled web as it is preserved and made available, followed by reflections on how some of the constitutive characteristics of the archived web outlined above play out with the crawled web, particularly with regard to incompleteness and temporal inconsistency.

7.2.3 The Crawled Web—a "Giant Bucket" of Files

The outcome of web crawling is a collection of HTML files, and of the files and services that are embedded or hyperlinked to. All files are either preserved as they were retrieved, or aggregated in archiving file formats such as ARC or WARC.

A crawled web collection may best be understood as a "giant bucket" with billions and billions of individual but potentially interlinked files. This means that the web archive may decide to take the files (or parts of them) out of the bucket again—and combine them—in a great variety of ways different from when the bits and pieces came in, including ways that by no means make the material appear as it looked when it was browsed in the past (see section 8.2). Therefore, a crawled web collection is malleable, and it may be made available in ways that may suit either general or highly specific researcher needs. This also means that there is no predetermined way of making the fragments available, but when this is done, it is always done in one specific way, or in several ways, each of which is a specific way of recombining the fragments and thereby reconstructing the already constructed, archived web.

A web collection may decide to reassemble the fragments so they resemble the way the web looked in a browser as much as possible when it was online. This is what is done with the Wayback software, the most commonly used display form for crawled web fragments and the form used by many major web archives. The web archive may also want to provide access to information about hyperlinks on the web pages, to support historical studies of hyperlink networks; then the web collection would not look like anything seen in a web browser, but would have the form of a file with hyperlink information only (such as a longitudinal graph analysis file (LGA)). Or image files could be singled out to support image analysis, and the collection would then have the form of a collection of this specific file type, either disconnected from the web pages where they originally sat, or with the option of relating each image to the website(s) of which it was part in the past. In any case, it is difficult to say which way best reflects the web that was once online. And the possibilities are almost infinite, which is why close collaboration between web collections and researchers is needed (see section 9.1).

It is evident that a collection with the foregoing characteristics may be made available in more—and more differentiated—ways than are possible with a digitized collection. Fragments are added to a digitized collection only at a later stage, if at all, such as in the form of OCR, whereas the crawled web collection is reborn fragmented and marked up, which offers an array of possible ways of making it accessible. However, this high level of flexibility of the crawled web collection comes at a price, since the collection's volatile nature also makes it a more malleable source than a digitized collection, where one file very often equals one copy of what was initially digitized (newspaper, radio program, etc.). In contrast, in a crawled web collection, files have to be patched together in ways that are not necessarily suggested by the archived original.

Finally, it has to be stressed that a crawled web collection also includes more than the archived files themselves, namely, the metadata files concerning what should be archived (seed list, definition of scope) and concerning how the archiving process actually went (crawl logs). In some cases, statistical information about what is in the collection is also included.

These metadata files are not always available to researchers, but in many cases they constitute important points of entry into the collection. In addition to the metadata files, which are closely related to the archiving process, other file types may be made available to provide yet other entry points, such as index files (e.g., CDX files) that may help determine what is in the collection, or derived data sets such as Web Archive Transformation files (WAT) with metadata information on what was archived, LGA files with hyperlink information, and Web Archive Named Entities files (WANE), with information on named entities.[2] Since these sorts of derived data sets are considerably smaller than the archived files, because they only hold a fraction of the information available in the files, they are particularly valuable when seeking to study large amounts of data.

That a collection's crawled web fragments are placed in the same "giant bucket" has an impact on two constitutive characteristics of the archived web—(in)completeness and temporal inconsistency—because they come in specific forms in a crawled collection.

7.2.4   The Crawled Web and (In)Completeness

In a digitized collection only one copy of each archived item usually exists, such as one copy of a handwritten document, newspaper, or radio program, and on a more detailed level, there is only one copy of each page, image, and so on, simply because there is only one in the original, and there is no good reason to have several identical copies when digitizing. And if we look at the online web, only one copy of each fragment exists at a certain point in time. But a collection of crawled web material is different in terms of completeness, because it is simultaneously incomplete and too complete. On the one hand, there is often too little in the collection, because all the fragments that were initially online may not have entered the archive, for the reasons previously mentioned, such as the choice of archiving form and strategy, the dynamics of updating, and technical deficiencies. Therefore, things may be missing from a crawled web collection for a variety of interacting reasons. And in some cases, this may affect the elements that were actually archived—for instance, if a style sheet for a web page was not archived, but all other elements were, then the preserved elements may be very difficult to display in a way that is close to the online original. On the other hand, there is often too much in the collection, because several versions of "the same" exist, which may be nearly identical, without being exactly identical. For example, the front page of a news website may have been archived at very short intervals, such as several times per day, or the same section of a website may have been archived every day. Thus, several (almost) identical versions from (almost) the same point in time may exist, and it may be very difficult to determine with certainty the extent to which they are identical, since they are versions. There may be several reasons for the existence of versions from (close to) the same point in time: a strategy close to "continuous" may have been chosen, whereby the many versions are the result of a deliberate choice, or the reason may be the online web's digitality as hyperlinked fragments combined with the web crawler's way of working, since its following hyperlinks may have led to the same web entity being accidently archived several times over a short time interval, if several hyperlinks pointed to it. Either way, the result is the same: there is too much material in the web archive compared to the online web and compared to a digitized collection, as though the front page of a newspaper from a given date was present in several almost identical versions, or as though some pages or images were identical in some versions and different in others.

The researcher using a web crawled collection is confronted with a messy patchwork of too little and too much of "the same" at the same time. Faced with such archived web entities that (partly) overlap in time and space— but without exact knowledge about what is actually the case—it may be difficult to establish how a given web entity may have looked when online in the past, or to evaluate unique versions. For instance, it may be possible to establish only how a given website looked in the past within a certain period of time, and not at an exact point in time, and in any case the reconstructed website is probably an assemblage that never existed in this form when initially online (see Brügger, 2005, p. 23).

7.2.5 The Crawled Web and Temporal Inconsistency

The fact that fragments are placed in the same bucket in a crawled web collection also affects temporal inconsistency, but in different ways, depending on how the fragments are made available.

Temporal inconsistency of a collection is seen in one of the most widespread ways of replaying the archived web, namely the Wayback Machine, the Internet Archive's instance of the Wayback software. This inconsistency takes a form that makes it almost imperceptible, but nevertheless it is there and affects the view of web elements and web pages, and by extension their possible use as historical sources for web history.

As previously mentioned (section 2.2), a web page on the online web that is shown in a web browser is patched together from bits and pieces retrieved from a web server (or web servers) at the time they are requested, based on the web page's HTML code. Something similar happens in the Wayback Machine, except that the bits and pieces are retrieved from the web archive's own collection rather than from an online web server. But if all the bits and pieces that should be patched together to form the web page the user wants to see in the archive are not available from the same date and time as the web page itself, the Wayback Machine's software retrieves the missing elements from a time as close as possible to the time of the web page. However, since this may be a question of days and in many cases weeks or months, the web page that the user sees, and that should be consistent with the time of the HTML file on the basis of which it is generated, is patched together from fragments from different points in time: a two-day-old banner ad, an image from the following week, and so on (see Ainsworth et al., 2015; Hockx-Yu, 2015).[3] What appears to be a temporally "flat" and consistent web page with only one temporality (as it was online) may hold several invisible temporalities, stretching backward and forward in time, making it temporally inconsistent as a whole. This is because of the fragmented nature of the crawled web and because all fragments— irrespective of when they were archived—are present at the same time in the same collection.[4]

In some web archives, the temporal inconsistency may have yet another consequence when the archived web is accessed through the Wayback software. As mentioned above, the Wayback Machine works like the online web, except that it retrieves files from its own collection, but this is only partly true. If a crawled web collection, such as the Internet Archive, is online and the Wayback Machine has to display a web page with a piece of HTML code that is supposed to contact a web server, and this web server is still online and can provide the requested content, the online content from the day the web archive is visited is shown as part of the web page. A weather forecast predicting snow when the web archive is visited during the summer may draw the user's attention to this temporal inconsistency caused by porous borders with the online web, but in other cases this may take place in subtler and less obvious ways. Online access to this type of web archive comes at the expense of not being separated from today's online web.[5] Therefore, a web page shown with the Wayback Machine may not only be temporally inconsistent within the archive, but may also be continuously inconsistent, since the web page will change concurrently with the changes to the online web.

The potential temporal inconsistency embedded in the Wayback Machine's view of an individual, browsable web page relates to web elements and web pages as presented in a web browser. But when focusing on other web strata, such as a website (but still seen through the Wayback Machine), or on other forms that make the crawled web available, the recognition and evaluation of the extent of any temporal inconsistency become more straightforward than with the Wayback Machine's subtle form of possible inconsistency on a web page level.

First, regarding the Wayback Machine's view used to combine web pages with entities bigger than the individual web page, such as a website, it works in a similar way to what happens on the page level, but in a more apparent way. If one clicks a hyperlink pointing to a web page on the same website, and this web page is not in the archive from the exact same date and time, the Wayback Machine presents the web page closest in time, and again, this time may be before or after the time of the page where one started. Thus, in these cases, the website as a whole becomes temporally inconsistent. Depending on how the Wayback Machine is configured, the exact time when the web page shown was archived is included as part of the URL address in the location bar, as is the case with the Internet Archive. This information is a great help to researchers evaluating the extent of the temporal inconsistency of an archived website.

Second, regarding other forms that make the crawled web available, these may include any form of extraction of archived fragments, either in the form of extraction of specific parts of an HTML file, such as hyperlinks, or in the form of specific file types themselves. In both cases, clear time stamps showing when things were archived can usually be made available, down to each individual fragment, which may provide valuable information about how consistent or inconsistent the material actually is. For instance, a longitudinal graph analysis file with extracted hyperlinks comes with information about the hyperlinks themselves and a time stamp indicating the time the page with the hyperlink was archived. It is then up to the researcher using the material to decide the degree of inconsistency that is acceptable, and to select the hyperlinks that will be used (see section 8.1).

The potential temporal inconsistency that existed at the time of archiving remains when the archived material is made available. But depending on the available forms of access, either it is not directly visible (as in the Wayback Machine's web page view), or it is visible in different forms, such as in the location bar in the Wayback Machine, or as a time stamp in a derived data file.

7.2.6   Web Preserved via an API

As previously mentioned, web crawling is not the only way to archive fragments, this also happens when the web is preserved and made accessible via an API. From the outset, material archived with an API is more ordered than the crawled web, because it follows a data structure provided by the data owner, and therefore it may be easier to preserve this material and make it available. But since it consists of fragments, this still allows for a great variety of ways of presenting the material to researchers, including ways that to some extent are independent of the data provider's data structure.

The possible temporal inconsistency of material retrieved via an API is different than it is in the crawled web. In general, inconsistency is a function of the fact that the archiving process took some time. In the case of the crawled web this is particularly challenging, because this archiving form is based on following hyperlinks, and therefore on as high a degree of consistency between link source and link target as possible. Therefore, the longer the time span of the crawling, the greater the potential temporal inconsistency. But in an API-based collection the fragments are not there as a result of an archiving process that takes time, but simply because they were created at a given point in time in the past, then retrieved with this time stamp at some later time. The fragments of a crawled web collection come with the time stamp of their archiving, whereas the fragments in an API collection come with the time stamp of their creation. Therefore, in terms of temporality, the API-based collection is as close as possible to the timeline of the online web of the past. And thus, when making the collection available, the potential temporal inconsistency is not a problem (provided that the details about time stamps or the API settings have not been changed at a later point in time; cf. section 5.3).

8   Scholarly Use of the Archived Web

Once the researcher who intends to do web history has found relevant versions of the old web, and has become familiar with the general and specific characteristics of the chosen collections, it is time to start studying the material.

The reborn web that is available to the researcher has already been constructed three times—when archived, when preserved, and when made available—and now follows a fourth form of construction, when the researcher starts to interact with the found material by making selections and analyzing them. And, just as the previous phases were functions of the ones preceding them, so too is the research phase where the archived web is actually used. Each of the interdependent choices previously made has, in its own way, set up an array of constraints and possibilities concerning the subsequent steps, and together they affect the shape of the last step, the research activity. The sum of each of the choices in the chain that provides the archived web to be studied impacts the extent to which the material makes it possible to perform the desired research and to answer the research questions.

Since this section is about the researchers' interactions with the archived web, the focus is on the nexus between the characteristics of the two general types of collections identified in section 7.2 ("What you see is what you can get" and "What you can get is what may be assembled"), on the one hand, and on the other hand, it is on a researcher's desire to study one or more specific web strata by focusing on either the visible or the hidden side of the strata in question. And since this is a matter of research, the phases that are usually part of any research process are included where relevant—that is, the selection of the material to be examined, followed by the creation of a corpus and the analysis itself.[1]

In brief, in the following paragraphs I discuss the challenges and possibilities that characterize web collections in general, and each of the two types of collections in particular, regarding how they enable selection, corpus creation, and analysis in relation to studies of the five web strata, where the focus is on either their visible or their hidden side (or both).

8.1 Constitutive Characteristics of Web Collections—Impact on Web History

Regardless of the type of collection of the archived web a researcher wants to study, the characteristics that are constitutive of any web collection have an impact on the research process (see section 7.1).

To illustrate the challenges and possibilities identified in this section, I sketch an imaginary research project. The project's overarching aim is to explore how American presidential candidates were portrayed in photographs and written text on candidate websites, news websites, and social media, in relation to the presidential elections in 1996, 2000, 2008, and 2016 (the analytical focus is on one web element—photographs—in their visible and hidden forms, and they are studied across the web sphere of websites). This small, imaginary example is used only to illustrate key points, and where relevant, the concrete cases of web history presented in chapter 4 will be referred to.

8.1.1 No Original to Go Back to, Incompleteness, and Unique Versions
The major challenge for any web history project is that the web of the past one wants to study may not be found in any existing web collection. But if relevant material is found, the next challenge is the fundamental uncertainty concerning the character of the archived web, which is an effect of the combination of the lack of an original, the fact that things are very likely to be missing, and the fact that what we find in a web collection are unique versions. Thus, although in many cases one has to be happy that some of the old web may be found at all, and therefore one must make do with what there is, the uncertainty of the archived web endows the research project with some uncertainty as to what is actually studied.

On a more detailed level, the fact that data are missing may not itself be a problem, if what is missing would not have been studied. If, for a study such as the one outlined above, images or hyperlinks cannot be found in a collection, this is a significant obstacle that may make the project impossible, at least based on this type of source material, but if sound files are missing, this is not that important. Therefore, incompleteness is always relative to the concrete research aim, and it is only a problem if the types of fragments that are missing would have been studied. Nevertheless, although incomplete source material is relative and is a problem familiar to any historian, the specific challenges related to web archives are different. Here the main problem is not only a possible lack of sources, but that the available sources may not be useful as they are, because it may be very difficult to evaluate the extent to which the available versions of any archived web entity are identical. Therefore, on the whole, the lack of an original, in combination with the possible incompleteness and the unique nature of versions, continuously threatens the reliability of the basic sources essential to any research project.

But although the digitality of the online web is one type of uncertainty that may sow doubt about the status of the archived web, it also suggests new possibilities that may even help to meet the above-mentioned challenges, at least to some extent. The reason for this is that what is missing may have left digital traces indicating its nature or may provide other sorts of information about what is actually found. For instance, an image file often contains information about when it was created, where and by whom, or other hidden data about its creation. HTML files may also provide valuable information about what would have been displayed. For example, the metadata tag may contain text stating what is on the web page or describing its creation, just as an embed or hyperlink code that refers to a missing image file may contain information about what was depicted in the image, such as the name of a person or locality. An example would be Raffal's study of the development of the websites related to Britain's armed forces, in which snippets of code were used to investigate missing content (Raffal, 2014 cf. section 4.3). And if the archiving is performed via web crawl, some of the metadata files may also provide information about what should have been archived. For instance, the seed list holds information about which web addresses were part of an instance of archiving; crawl logs tell a lot about what was intended to be archived but did not go into the archive, and they even have information that may suggest some possible reasons for this.

Although material is missing in the archive, what is there may help to establish the greater picture of how a given web entity may have looked or what it consisted of, and this sort of information may also constitute a stepping-stone for searching for the missing digital objects in other collections. The methods used in such detailed studies may in many ways be similar to those of philology, where pieces of a manuscript may be used to reconstruct an entire manuscript, although there are also differences between philology and web philology (see section 9.2). But it is fair to maintain that although some aspects of the digitality of the archived web may present challenges for the web historian, other elements may offer strategies for meeting the challenges. And in this respect, collections of the archived web are different from digitized collections, first, because establishing what is digitized is usually not a problem, and second, because in many cases, digitized collections are not born with a markup textual layer that may help when investigating what is missing.

When it comes to corpus creation, the presence of "too much" in a web collection may present a challenge, since several versions of nearly the same web entity may exist. This means that when constructing a corpus, this must be done in two steps; first an initial corpus is delimited in time and space, and then the versions that should be included have to be selected. Thus, a web archive corpus tends to be a double construction, in contrast to a corpus on the online web, where one web address equals one web entity at a given point in time.

8.1.2 Possible Temporal and Spatial Inconsistency between the Archived Fragments

The temporal and spatial inconsistencies between the archived fragments, which may exist in any collection of the archived web, present a challenge to any study that intends to focus on relationships between fragments, which de facto usually means including hyperlinks in the study.

If a project such as the one outlined above, where the aim is to examine the hyperlink network between images on the websites of presidential candidates, is based on a collection of websites that spans many months, it is very likely that link sources and link targets are not archived at the same time, or that some link targets are not archived at all. This will mean that, when analyzed, if a link source archived on one day points to a link target archived a week later, the content of the latter, including its hyperlinks, is likely to have changed. Thus, first, what was linked to is not the same entity and images that were there may have disappeared, and, second, if the hyperlinks on the page linked to are also to be included in hyperlink analysis as link sources pointing to yet other link targets, these targets may have been archived even later, and so on. And if this simple scenario is multiplied, it is no surprise that the network analysis as such becomes biased or imprecise, because it is not performed within a very limited time frame, as is the case on the online web. Instead it takes place within an extended time frame, possibly with overlapping temporalities, which will be very difficult to account for if used as is. Even evaluating if, how, and how much of a problem this is may be challenging.

Something similar to the foregoing may happen in terms of spatial extension, if a study is based on a collection in which the websites of one candidate were archived in depth, including all levels below the front page, whereas other candidates' websites had only the front page or maybe a couple of levels of the website archived. In this case, the material would be spatially inconsistent, and if, for instance, the analysis was intended to focus on the use of images on all candidates' entire websites, the analysis would be biased if such material was used.

These above-mentioned inconsistencies mean that any subsequent analysis, for example of the hyperlink network, may be based on either a temporally inconsistent collection of link sources and link targets, or on a spatially inconsistent set of web pages from varying depths—or both.[2] In both cases, there are no good solutions for overcoming these challenges, only strategies for handling and minimizing the problems in ways where one has to balance the need for consistency against the need for having something to study. When creating a corpus, a general rule applies regarding temporal inconsistency. One may select a short period of time, which will reduce the possible temporal inconsistency, while probably also reducing the amount of material to be studied. Or a longer interval may be chosen, which will increase the likelihood of temporal inconsistency, while probably also increasing the amount of material to be included (however, probably also increasing the number of overlapping but not identical versions). The presence of time stamps may help with this, but only for discovering how consistent or inconsistent things are. How this trade-off is to be negotiated depends on the particular research project and what is available in a given collection.

With regard to spatial inconsistency, it is not possible to proceed as with temporal inconsistency, mainly because of the lack of something similar to a time stamp that could help to determine the spatial extent of the individual web entities. Thus, since what was not archived cannot be retrieved, one way forward is to reduce the amount of the archived web to the same level (e.g., only front pages), which comes at the expense of possibly relevant material that may be excluded.

In relation to both temporal and spatial inconsistencies in the source material, choices have to be made concerning how good or bad a source may be to be acceptable. For instance, the possible role of the inconsistencies may be less important, the greater the amount of data being studied. As often maintained in big data studies, inexactitude is frequently an unavoidable consequence of large-scale data. As Mayer-Schönberger and Cukier note, we may have to shift the analytical goal in a more general direction than knowing every detail of a phenomenon: "With big data, we'll often be satisfied with a sense of general direction rather than knowing a phenomenon down to the inch, the penny, the atom" (Mayer-Schönberger & Cukier, 2013, p. 13). But in any case, it may be difficult to make informed choices, because, as mentioned, it is difficult to obtain a reliable overview of the extent of the problem.

To complicate matters, if a study needs to compare web material from several years, such as developments related to presidential elections in 1996, 2000, 2008, and 2016, the researcher may have to deal with what may be termed "the inconsistency of inconsistencies"—that is, the fact that for each of those years, different link sources, link targets, and web pages may be missing or may exist in several versions. The inconsistency of inconsistencies may challenge a systematic comparison that maps developments.

8.2 Two Collection Types and Their Impact on Web History

The researcher's use of web collections is affected by the constitutive cross-collection characteristics outlined above and the characteristics of the two general types of collections previously identified—that is, collections of "What you see is what you can get" and collections of "What you can get is what may be assembled." In the following paragraphs, some of the challenges and possibilities that characterize researchers' potential use of each of these two collection types are debated, while still keeping in mind the imagined use case of how American presidential candidates are portrayed in photographs and written text on candidate websites (mentioned at the beginning of section 8.1).

8.2.1   Studying a "What You See Is What You Can Get" Collection

A researcher who intends to study the use of images and written text on the websites of presidential candidates has found a collection of screen dumps, files with individual web pages, and a few screen movies. If the researcher wants to include the visible side of the candidate websites, she faces a number of challenges. First, this type of source material is not easy to search in any systematic and detailed way; files with individual web pages may be searched individually, but as for the rest, the only way of finding relevant material is to go through all the sources manually. In particular, screen movies may be challenging to navigate, since they follow the actions of the individual who did the filming. Second, combining web pages to form an entire website is challenging to do consistently, and even obtaining an overview of the pages' interrelations may be difficult, mainly because the hidden code level is not accessible. Third, in cases where hyperlinks are to be studied, it is a great disadvantage that the code level is not available, since the existence of hyperlinks is not always expressed in any immediately visible way, but may be experienced only when a cursor is placed over the link source (therefore, hyperlinks may be visible in screen movies). Fourth, in terms of possible forms of analysis, the most obvious way of analyzing this type of material is traditional manual image analysis, as would be done with any other type of image. Finally, because of the manual approach in both search and analysis, research projects based on images and movies do not scale well.

Despite the foregoing challenges, screen dumps, files with individual web pages, and screen movies also come with some important advantages. First, and most importantly, the images and movies show (by and large) exactly how the web entities looked, thus providing the "look and feel" of the past web. For instance, images are displayed and positioned correctly on the web pages, screenshots may show how several open web pages relate if they display several open browser windows in the same image, and a social media feed may document a rapidly changing content flow. This advantage has been an important condition for the type of web history study that focuses on how websites actually looked, such as Engholm's style history study (Engholm, 2002) or Rogers's screencast documentary of Google's front page (Rogers, 2013) (see section 4.2). Second, creating a corpus and preserving it is relatively simple and straightforward; it may be done by simply creating the needed folders on a desktop. Third, although the form of the material tends to enhance reading the text as one would do in a nondigital medium, automated textual analyses cannot be ruled out. Since screenshots are bitmaps, they may be enriched with OCR, and as for individual web pages saved as pdfs, it is possible to make a simple copy of the text and paste it in another file format. Fourth, although the most obvious way of approaching the images is manually, by looking at them one by one, one should not forget that the image files are, in fact, digital images, and therefore they may also be analyzed based on automated image recognition—for example, to determine the ratio between photographs and written text on each web page. This is exactly what Cocciolo has done in his study of how the quantity of written text develops over time (see Cocciolo, 2015, presented in greater detail in section 4.1). Therefore, if automated methods are applied, a research project based on image files and the like may, in fact, scale. Fifth, although the most obvious approach to screen images of web pages tends to be to look at them one by one, other presentation forms may be used, at least as stepping-stones to an analysis, namely, the display forms mentioned in section 3.3 that can show a large number of images, either as an image wall or as a collage that allows zooming in/out. Such tools are enabled because the screen images are in digital form, and they may help establish an overview of a large collection.

If a researcher did not want to analyze the visible side but instead intended to focus on the hidden text—that is, the HTML code and associated files, for instance with a view to making a hyperlink analysis or calculating the number of image files embedded in each web page—the "What you see is what you can get" type of source material is obviously of little use. In short, these types of studies are impossible, based on this material.

In summary, a collection of screen dumps, files with individual web pages, and screen movies has to be approached in much the same way as any other collection of digital images and films, and therefore the historiographic methods usually used for this type of material are probably the most effective approach. However, as outlined above, automated methods may be considered.

8.2.2 Studying a "What You Can Get Is What May Be Assembled" Collection

If the researcher who wants to study presidential candidates' websites in relation to presidential elections in 1996, 2000, 2008, and 2016 has found a collection of the crawled web, or has access to material retrieved via API, this presents new challenges and creates other possibilities. In the following paragraphs, a crawled collection's possible impact on research is debated—first as used in research focused on the visible web, second if the focus is on the visible/hidden, and, third, if the focus is on the hidden side of the web—followed by reflections on the problems related to a collection established via API.

8.2.3 Studying the Visible Web Text

For the researcher who wants to analyze the visible side of a given web stratum, the fundamental challenge presented by a web-crawled collection is that the visible web strata have not been archived as such. The researcher does not have immediate access to how the web of the past actually looked. On the contrary, what is accessible is the previously mentioned "giant bucket" of possibly interlinked bits and pieces originating from the web of the past (see section 7.2), but they have to be assembled to form something that resonates with how the online web may have looked. One way of doing this is with the Wayback Machine. Therefore, the researcher studying the visible layer is, in fact, studying the hidden layer as made visible by the Wayback Machine—that is, the hidden layer is indirectly part of the analysis of the visible layer.

The use of the Wayback Machine affects the steps of the research process in various ways. The first thing is the search, and here the main challenge is that the Wayback Machine does not allow for entry points other than the web address, the URL. This means that if the researcher does not know the URL, it is impossible to find the relevant material to study. The reason for this is that the Wayback Machine is basically a replay tool that patches together the bits and pieces to form something as close as possible to the way the online web looked. However, some web archives have made it possible to browse the collection by subject (such as the Australian PANDORA), and others have created indexes that allow for full text search (of all or parts of the material), such as the Internet Archive, the UK Web Archive, the Portuguese Web Archive, and the Danish Netarkivet. In cases where this is combined with user interfaces that allow for the filtering of results (e.g., by file type, year, or post code), this creates new possibilities for researcher engagement with these web collections.[3] But full text search also comes with some challenges that distinguish the crawled web from many other collection types. In a digitized collection, presenting search results is relatively simple, because typically there is only one copy of each entity from any given point in time—a newspaper, a radio program—but with a web archive it may be a challenge to present large numbers of search results where many of the results are nearly identical (and may overlap) in any meaningful way that allows for further exploration of the material. And if access to the found web page is needed, as would be the case in a study of the visible side of presidential websites, search results will ultimately lead to the result being replayed in the Wayback Machine.

Once the relevant web pages are found—either by URL, full text search, or other—and they are shown in the Wayback Machine, they are displayed one by one, each possibly having an embedded temporal inconsistency, as previously described. That is, the inconsistency would originate in other elements already in the web collection, or from outside the web archive if the collection is connected to the online web (section 7.2). It is evident that doubts about whether a web page contains an embedded temporal inconsistency present a challenge to any researcher wanting to make claims concerning the exact way a given web page looked in the past. But the possible remedy may be near at hand, because with the crawled web the code is available, and therefore it is possible to check the time stamps of each individual web element on a web page to determine the extent of temporal drift. However, this is a time-consuming task that does not scale, but it can probably be automated and maybe even shown as part of the display of the web page, similar to what the Memento Time Travel does (see section 7.2.5). But instead of showing how a given web page may be patched together from bits and pieces originating in different web archives, it could show how a given web page is actually patched together from bits and pieces from one web archive. However, despite the possible inconsistencies, the many advantages offered by the Wayback Machine's presentation should not be forgotten, most notably that researchers have access to a browsable web page with the look and feel of the old web, and with working hyperlinks, although the challenges are just below the surface. The Wayback Machine may not show the correct look and feel if, for instance, images or a style sheet keeping the elements in place are missing, and hyperlinks may well make the user jump in time with each click.

As mentioned, the Wayback Machine shows individual web pages one by one, which is why it may be a challenge to establish how a given website looked, since the web page is, if not the archival unit, then the display unit. Therefore, to establish how a website looked in the past, the researcher has to browse through all the interlinked web pages that form the website. But keeping the previously mentioned temporal inconsistency between web pages in mind—the fact that a click may take the user backward and forward in time, depending on what was archived, and when—it is evident that a study of the web strata of the website is challenging. And the more websites are included—for instance, presidential candidates' websites to form a web sphere—the messier the network of different and partly overlapping temporalities.

The display format of the Wayback Machine makes it challenging to establish a consistent corpus to study on web strata bigger than the individual web page, let alone the practical challenge of handling such a corpus in the Wayback view, even if it consists of web pages only. What is needed is some sort of researcher interface that allows for the clustering of the web pages found in the Wayback Machine, as such or as they are considered to be forming a website in a given time period.

If a corpus of web pages has been identified in the Wayback Machine, then the researcher's next step would be to analyze the material, and since the focus is on the visible side only, historiographic approaches and methods that are usually employed with this type of source may be used, while continuously keeping a methodological eye on the above-mentioned peculiarities of the material. But since the sources are in the form of individual web pages as viewed in the Wayback Machine, the scale of the analysis should probably be limited.

The Wayback software is by far the most widespread way of presenting the visible crawled web to researchers, but other forms exist, such as a scrollable wall with a selection of a collection's holdings, as seen in the UK Web Archive. But although presentation forms such as this display the visible web, it is shown as a static image of what is in the archive, and not in a browsable form, as in the Wayback Machine.

8.2.4 Studying the Visible and the Hidden Web Text

As mentioned above, the researcher studying the visible layer of the web is, in fact, studying the hidden layer as well, although only indirectly. In contrast to the indirect inclusion of the hidden layer via the Wayback Machine, the researcher may also want to include the hidden layers more directly, even when studying the visible layer. For instance, the inclusion of the HTML code may reveal relevant information about the images, such as whether embedded images are retrieved from web servers other than the one hosting the website, just as access to the actual hyperlink commands could shed new light on the hyperlink network and make it easier to analyze it. But proceeding in this way also comes with a set of challenges, the major one being how to operationalize the visible object of study as something that may be studied in the code. As pointed out in section 3.3, in some cases going from a visible web element to a corresponding web element in the code may be a relatively trivial task, for instance finding out whether images originate from the same web server as the website. But in other cases, operationalizing a research interest on the visible level may not be that straightforward, for instance when studying colors or the use of landscape and portrait formats for photographs.

Supplementing an analysis of what was visible on web pages based on the Wayback Machine's view, with the inclusion of the code, is not necessarily helpful; nevertheless, it offers new options. In relation to the search, the inclusion of the code may add new dimensions, such as when information not displayed in the Wayback Machine is included, like metatags, geographic information, and so on. As mentioned above, referring to time stamps of individual web elements—that is, another element of code—may help determine the degree of temporal inconsistency of a presented web page, just as similar information may be useful when setting out to evaluate the temporal drift on the website and web sphere strata. When it comes to missing elements on a web page, the code may also be helpful. For example, if a style sheet is missing, causing the web elements to be haphazardly positioned without specific fonts for headings and such, information about the style sheet may make it possible to locate the correct style sheet in other files from the same website, where it may have been archived. Finally, when it comes to analyzing the visible material, including the code may be helpful. If one manages to transform and operationalize what is investigated on the visible level to code, it is possible to supplement analyses of the visible with automated analyses. For instance, a researcher could conduct a hyperlink analysis of the images of presidential candidates' websites, based on hyperlink information in the code, but showing the actual images that are interlinked, possibly in the context of the web pages where they were located. In this way, an analysis of the visible archived web may be scaled up, in contrast to an analysis that includes web pages only as viewed in the Wayback Machine.

8.2.5   Studying the Hidden Web Text

A researcher intending to study presidential websites in 1996, 2000, 2008, and 2016 may not want to analyze the visible side at all. The source of such a study would then be the hidden text only, without any attention paid to how the images and websites actually looked when online in the past. For instance, this could be a study of the hyperlink network, the number of specific file types, streamed video, or the use of blog software (for typical examples of historical studies based on hyperlink code, see chapter 4). These types of studies also come with a range of challenges as well as possibilities.

In contrast to studies of the visible web strata, which access the code and associated files only indirectly, mainly through the Wayback Machine, studies based on only the hidden code must have access to the HTML files themselves (often as compiled in ARC/WARC files), or to relevant extractions of archived fragments, such as information about metadata, hyperlinks, or named entities (e.g., in WAT, LGA, and WANE files, respectively). For instance, access to a file with all links on the UK web year by year played an important role in many studies of the development of the UK web (see the studies mentioned in chapter 4 based on the "JISC UK Web Domain Dataset (1996–2013)"). Or one must have access to information in metadata files such as seed lists, crawl logs, or statistics where this is relevant for the study.

When studying only the hidden side of the web the phases of an investigation look different than when studying the visible side of the web. Searches of the invisible text and its fragments in a crawled web collection come in forms other than URL and full text searches as known from the Wayback Machine. Such search forms are not available for all web collections, but if they exist it is usually in the form of access to a file with the index that the Wayback software uses when looking up which bits and pieces to combine in the web page view (a CDX file). For instance, the

Internet Archive and the Portuguese Web Archive provide online access to their CDX files through an open API, which supports users with information about URLs, time stamps, and file types, among other things, and it is possible to filter by time range or other parameters. Other types of indexes may exist, such as the index enabling the full text search where this is available, but this is usually only accessible through the full text search interface. Also, if there are derived data sets with metadata (WAT file), hyperlink information (LGA), or information about named entities (WANE), they may be searchable as such. Finally, if the above-mentioned metadata files, such as seed lists or crawl logs, are available, they may also be queried, but access to this information is rarely provided by web archives. These forms of searches may present a challenge, in the sense that handling the search process and the search results requires the establishment of some sort of data structure, either at the web archive or at the researcher's end, but there is no doubt that they offer the opportunity to access large amounts of archived web material in machine-readable form.

The impact of the characteristics of the archived web as seen in the Wayback Machine on the researcher's use of the visible level does not disappear when moving to the hidden level, primarily because the fragments that are assembled in the Wayback Machine originate in the hidden level—that is, what was initially archived. Thus, the material may still be incomplete (or too complete, or both) and temporally inconsistent. But in contrast to the Wayback Machine's page view, inconsistencies are, on the one hand, more obvious, since they are not embedded in a view form that appears as a web page generated at a single point in time or web pages that apparently form a temporally coherent website. Instead, they come in the form of a clear time stamp related to each archived fragment. On the other hand, it may be harder to decide how to handle the temporal inconsistencies. For example, if in an analysis of the hyperlink network a given link source points to a given link target from three different points in time, it is not obvious which one should be selected. This might be easily determined if the link targets were viewed, but when the focus is exclusively on the code level, such decisions have to be automated, which may make the results in each case less clear.

It is possible to search and provide access to the code level of a crawled web collection by archiving what is already archived, which may be accomplished with web archives that are accessible online, such as the Internet

Archive. In this case, a range of URLs are queried in the web archive, and then the relevant content is downloaded and preserved as code, ready to be analyzed. Typical examples of studies where this approach is used are Weltevrede and Helmond's study of the development of the Dutch blogosphere, and Helmond's investigation of the history of trackers on the *New York Times* website (see Weltevrede and Helmond, 2012, and Helmond, 2017, presented in sections 4.4 and 4.6).

It may be challenging to create a corpus based on the above-mentioned forms of access to the web collections. Although an index of the collection's holdings or archived URLs, such as a CDX file, enables searches of the holdings, going from identifying the websites of presidential candidates one wants to study to the material itself as preserved in a collection is not straightforward. For instance, if the aim is to study the written text on all web pages, access to the body text is needed, and in most web archives it is not possible to obtain this in its HTML form, but only as displayed in its visible form in the Wayback Machine. Derived data sets may be searched; they usually hold only the data that were initially derived, and not the data of the entire collection from which they originate, although this may be the case for smaller collections. For instance, if an LGA file with hyperlinks related to dog breeding has been created based on a much larger collection, this list is probably not of much use if one wants to study the hyperlink networks related to presidential candidates' websites. But if a derived data set with hyperlinks of the entire collection exists, this will allow the researcher to make the necessary selections to make it fit her research project.

Selecting a range of URLs in a CDX index or in another of the above-mentioned file types may be a first step in creating a corpus, and in some cases this will be enough to support the study. But in other cases it is necessary to have access to what is actually in the archive—that is, the HTML files (potentially as stored in WARC files).

If a researcher has succeeded in creating the corpus she needs, the data analysis follows, and this is where the possibilities of the archived web's digitality outweigh the challenges it presents, simply because a corpus based on the above formats is machine-readable. Therefore the analysis may be automated, so analyses of large amounts of data are possible, and the analysis may focus on each type of archived fragment that is expressed in the code, thereby making the analysis very fine-grained. Thus, analyses of presidential candidates' websites may easily include millions of images and thousands of web pages. Finally, in relation to this type of analysis, the previously mentioned point about operationalization from one web layer to the other should again be emphasized, but in its reverse form. When analyzing only the hidden level, the question is how this analytical object translates into what happens in the visible layer. For example, what is the relation between the machine-readable hyperlinks and the nodes actually shown on web pages?

8.2.6 Studying the Web as It Is Made Accessible via API

The researcher who wants to study the development of presidential candidates' websites may also have gained access to the old web that is accessible via API. This sort of source material also has its challenges and possibilities. If the researcher wants to analyze the visible side of the websites in question, all the elements may be there, and in their original forms, but they are not combined to form the web page or the website as they have looked in the past. And in contrast to what is done by the Wayback Machine, usually it is not possible to reconstruct the web page in which the elements were shown. But the bits and pieces are there, and may be analyzed as such, and since they come in a structured form, as they were supplied by the content owner, this makes it easier to search and filter the material, and to create a corpus and perform analyses. Particularly for studies of feeds of status updates on social media, it is a great advantage to have all the updates in a structured form and with the time stamps of their creation, compared to the crawled web, where such content is usually not preserved in its totality. Also, given the characteristics of the web preserved via API, all the steps of the research process are scalable. However, the possible ways of performing these steps may be limited, if the researcher does not access the material directly via the content provider's API but has to use it in the form it was collected and preserved in by another archiving actor, such as a vendor or a research group.

In case the researcher does not intend to focus on the web as it looked, but wants to map the hyperlink network between images on different websites, the structured form of web material archived via API offers a number of possibilities for performing large-scale and fine-grained analyses based on the web elements themselves. This may also include fragments that were not shown on the web page once it was online, such as information about geolocation, or the device from which the material was accessed (laptop, smartphone, etc.). However, in either case the possible incompleteness of the material must be considered.

8.3   Cross-Collection Studies

In any historical study it is not unusual for sources from various collections to be used, and this is also the case when doing web history, including collections of the archived web. However, using the archived web from different collections or types of collections also comes with challenges and possibilities.

If in a research project on the websites of presidential candidates, archived web material has been found in different collections, it is very likely that these collections may vary in many respects, from differences in archiving forms and strategies, to different ways of preserving and providing access. Thus, given these differences, a major challenge is to combine the found material.

If an analysis is focused on the visible elements of websites and it is based on screenshots, files with individual web pages, or screen movies, collections may easily be combined. But if it is based on the crawled web—with a view to studying either the visible or the hidden sides—it may be challenging to combine collections. There may be legal and technical obstacles, in terms of obtaining access, and there may be differences in forms of access and standards. Extracting a corpus from each collection could be one way forward, but not all collections allow for this, and taking an extraction out of an archive may not be possible either. Also, the number of versions will probably grow, which will add to the already existing challenge of evaluating versions in each collection, and the result may be far too many versions with possible inconsistencies. Therefore, the interoperability of web archives presents a challenge that tends to increase with the number of collections involved. The major advantage of combining collections should also be emphasized, namely, that having as complete a set of sources as possible may help to improve the research project. For example, the different collections may supplement one another, as seen in the presentation in chapter 4 of Mataly's study on how web material related to Margaret Thatcher was archived (Mataly, 2013), and in Nanni's study of the development of the unibo.it website (Nanni, 2017).

9 Toward a Source Criticism of the Archived Web

Web historians who set out to base their research on the archived web should start by acknowledging that, although at first sight an archived web collection may look like a digitized collection or the online web, it is fundamentally different from both, and thus must be approached differently.

It is important to become familiar with the specific digitality of any archived web collection one uses for research purposes, by procuring as much information as possible about its provenance, and by determining how the general characteristics of the archived web play out in each collection. Then one can make the most informed choices possible as to selecting and creating a corpus to study, as well as performing the analysis in each case. And—most importantly—it is essential to continuously explain and document these methodological reflections about the nature and provenance of the material. In many ways, these steps parallel traditional historiographic skills. But the concrete work with the sources comes in new forms because of the digitality of the archived web, which requires that traditional approaches be reinterpreted and translated to fit the new conditions.

Part of such methodological reflections is evaluating the reliability of a source of the archived web, including comparing different versions with a view to getting as close as possible to establishing what may have been online in the past. In doing this one should use methods that facilitate the critical investigation of the archived web as a source (see section 1.2). In many respects, such a venture resembles philological work involving variants of handwritten manuscripts, but there are also major differences, mainly because of the digitality of the archived web. Whereas the previous chapter focused on the challenges and possibilities related to researcher engagement with the archived web, this chapter reflects on some of the methodological steps that may help the web historian who is starting to interact with and analyze instances of the archived web. Thus, this chapter will outline a few elements to possibly include in a future source criticism of the archived web.

Before exploring this source criticism in greater detail, it is important to reflect on what characterizes the new field of interaction that is established between web archives and researcher communities, because to some extent this area constitutes the conditions for possible researcher interaction with the archived web.

9.1   Researcher Interaction with Collections—Negotiating Forms of Access

Collections have to be made available to their users, including researchers. With nondigital collections, the ways of doing this were relatively limited. Typically, the medium (book, newspaper, cassette, etc.) or artifact could be searched for and then handed over to the researcher to be studied, which was usually done in the same way, regardless of who the researcher was and what the research project addressed. With digitized collections this changes a bit, because more sophisticated search facilities are developed. Also, if collections are online, there is usually a direct link to the digital object, and in many cases, what is found in the collection may be downloaded in various formats for study.

With the archived web, and in particular the crawled web and the web retrieved by API, the scenario above changes dramatically, because of the digitality of the online web and of the archived web. What are archived are marked-up fragments, and since they are preserved in a "giant bucket" as fragments, they may be taken out and reassembled in a great variety of ways. Therefore, choosing which forms of accessibility collections should offer is not a matter of choosing among a limited number of search filters and download formats, it is a matter of getting an idea of the many forms of access that are possible, and then choosing to provide some of them. However, making these choices may be very difficult for the collection owner, because in contrast to the situation that exists in a nondigital collection, and in part also in a digitized collection, it is not a matter of providing the same form of access, regardless of who the researcher is and what the research project is about. On the contrary, the malleable nature of the archived web offers an array of possible ways of interacting with the archived web fragments, each of which may be a function of a specific researcher interest, and thus it may to be tailored to fit this.

What is offered by the archived web is a new, flexible, and complex field of interaction between collections of the archived web and the research communities—a field of collaboration where the forms of access may be negotiated, while still balancing the technical, organizational, legal, and resource constraints of the web archive against different researcher communities' needs and requirements for tailored forms of access.[1] And in contrast to other types of collections (including other digital collections) these negotiations are ongoing, given the great variety of possibilities, and if they do not take place, the full research potential of the material may not be exploited, or the material may be made available in ways that are not useful for researchers. The challenge for web collection holders is to strike the right balance between providing generic forms of access that may be used by as many as possible, and forms of access that are tailored to fit very few research projects.

Since the possible forms of access provision are closely linked to the steps that the collections take before providing access, such as the web archiving forms and strategies, the collaboration could with advantage span the entire web archiving workflow, and even beyond, since organizational structures are needed to support the life cycle of research data management. Given the character of the archived web, it is not necessarily clear whether such services should be hosted by the web archives, by the research communities, or by something in between, either new institutions or collaborations.

When debating the methodological considerations related to the use of the archived web, the foregoing conditions are important to bear in mind, because to some extent evaluating its potential use for research is a function of how the field of access provision is negotiated. The tools necessary to address such concerns as source criticism and versions have to be established by the web collections in collaboration with the research communities. In this sense, researcher involvement must be an inherent part of a web collection if it is to be useful, because the traditional approaches used when studying other source types need to be replicated by other means in a web archive.

9.2 Interacting with the Archived Web as a Source

In many ways, the web historian's work resembles that of any historian, except that in the cases where the archived web is included as a source—be it in writing history with the web or of the web—the traditional skills and methods may have to be supplemented with approaches that reflect the digitality of the archived web, as already noted in section 1.2. In the following paragraphs, the focus is on some of the topics that are important when working with sources in general, such as provenance, how to create an overview, how to evaluate versions, and how to reference. Not all topics necessarily apply to all forms of the archived web, or relate to all research projects. Instead, they may be considered a catalog of possible things to consider and suggestions for how to proceed.

9.2.1 Provenance

As with any other source type, it is important for web historians to have the most exact knowledge possible about the provenance of what is being studied, including information about what the source is, who created it and with what purpose, where it comes from, and when it was created.

It may be both easy and difficult to provide information about the provenance of the simplest forms of the archived web, such as screenshots, files of individual web pages, or screen movies. If the material is found in an established web collection such as the UK Web Archive or a self-described web museum, some information about provenance may be provided, but in many other cases, establishing provenance may be difficult, in particular if the material is found on the World "Wild" Web. For instance, it is usually difficult to date screenshots based on the image file itself (although in some cases date information may be part of the file), but then the historiographic methods usually used may be applied, such as establishing a timeline based on other sources that may be dated, and then using this as a reference. For example, this method was used in a study of the textual development of Facebook (see the presentation in chapter 4 of Brügger, 2015).

With a crawled web collection, the researcher is in many ways reasonably well positioned to establish the provenance of an archived web entity, at least in principle, since most of the relevant provenance information is there. But that the information is available is not tantamount to its being immediately accessible, and thereby useful to researchers. Mainly, provenance information may exist in some of the metadata that are created as part of the processes of archiving and displaying archived content—that is, documents outlining the decisions about what should be archived, the crawl log, and CDX files. Documents about archiving decisions exist in various forms, some of which are formal and written down, whereas others are of a more informal nature. Examples of the first are documents that specify the overall archiving strategies and describe how they should be executed to fulfill their goals, whereas the latter may be documents shared among curators about the choices that were made, or the concrete scope settings for each web crawl. Whereas strategies and rules concerning scope give information about what was intended to be crawled, the crawl log is a log file that records what actually happened once the web crawl was started, which is by no means always what was intended to happen. The crawl log holds information about all the steps that the web crawler performed while trying to archive the URLs that it was supposed to archive, including information about the initial seed URLs, errors encountered, when the archiving started and stopped, redirects and blocked web content, and the discovery path—that is, how the web crawler reached a given web entity. Finally, the CDX files hold information about the content that actually went into the web archive, including each URL and time stamp. All this information may comprise a treasure trove for web historians who are trying to establish the provenance of what is in a web archive, what should have been archived, why it did end up there, and when. Unfortunately, this type of information is only rarely made available to researchers, except for CDX files, which are available via open API from some of the web archives that are online.

Since the metadata files are mainly inaccessible in most web archives, at least for the time being, one must make do with what is available, which in most cases is replay via the Wayback software. Usually only the date is shown (as part of the archive URL in the location bar), but since the Wayback software displays HTML files, it is always possible to switch to the HTML code, where some information about what is being viewed may be found, just as information about who created the HTML page and such may be available. And if the previously mentioned Memento Time Travel is used, it is possible to see exactly which bits and pieces are patched together to form a given web page.

Finally, it should be emphasized that a number of web archives come with metadata of a more traditional nature, such as information about the subject, genre, and description, as seen in the Library of Congress web archive, or the set archiving intervals, as seen in the Australian PANDORA.

In general, well-documented information about the archived web, presented in a form that is useful for researchers, is scarce.

9.2.2 Creating an Overview

Once the provenance of what one wants to study has been established to the extent possible, in many cases it will make sense to establish some sort of overview of what is included in the selected web material. For instance, this would include any kind of registry or directory that can contain a great variety of information about the specific elements of study—such as web elements or web pages—but usually such a registry will have at least basic information about the name or title of the entity being studied, the spatial extent of what is registered, and a date.

With a web archive, establishing even a very simple overview may not be as straightforward as it is for other types of collections, including a digitized collection. The main reason for this is that what is meant by "name," "spatial extent," and "date" may be more complicated to define than it is for other media types (it is most complicated with the crawled web, but in principle, this affects all archiving forms).

Most lists used to establish an overview include the name or title of what will be registered. In a digitized collection of newspapers or radio programs this could be the name of the newspaper (or the title of an article), or the title of the program, and in general, this information is provided by the institution, company, or whoever else has produced it. Web content does not come with the same clearly marked names or titles, and in many cases, no precise names are provided, if names are provided at all. One may choose the URL in the location bar—the URL is always there, also in a web archive (at least for crawled collections)—but a list of page URLs may easily become confusing. The title of individual web pages that may be viewed in the browser may also be used, but web pages do not always come with titles, and in many cases they are useless as unique identifiers, so a third approach would be to provide a title oneself, based on the content of the web page. If the entity to be registered is a website, all three types of names are possible, although the URL may be the most obvious, but all sections of a website may not share the same URL. Also, it is quite common for a website to have many URLs, namely in cases where the website owner owns several domain names, each of which redirects to the website's front page. Since the order of website and redirect may change over time, just as new redirecting URLs may be added or some may be deleted, using the URL as the name of an archived entity has some shortcomings.

In contrast to digitized collections, where what is registered is usually clearly delimited in space, either by the medium's spatial extension (e.g., a copy of a newspaper), by clear semiotic markers (e.g., a radio program), or by combinations (e.g., a newspaper article), not all forms of the archived web come with clear, built-in spatial demarcations. What is most clearly delimited is the web page, since it may be understood as whatever is present in a browser window, in many ways similar to the page of a newspaper. And a web element on a web page may also be delimited, similar to a photograph on a newspaper page. But when it comes to the website, borders are less clearly defined, mainly because a website is constituted by interrelated web pages that are interrelated semantically, formally, and in physically performative ways (see section 3.1). But since these delimitations are not directly functions of the outer limits of the medium's material characteristics (like an article in a newspaper being printed on the page), in principle, an endless number of web pages may be added to a website, and they do not all have to be interlinked to all the others. And since they are not unfolding in linear time only (like the radio program), delimiting a website in space is less fixed, and it may change over time. Therefore, deciding exactly what entity will be listed in a registry is also less determined beforehand.

Finally, there are differences in the archived web's temporal extension, in comparison to that of a digitized collection. Newspapers and radio programs are clearly positioned in time, either by a point in time, such as a newspaper with a date of publication (or hour) or a program with a start and end time, and a register of such material will usually use this temporal information. Individual archived web pages were also archived at specific points in time, and therefore, despite the fact that when displayed by the Wayback software they may be patched together from fragments from different times, the time of archiving is still a relevant entry point for a register of web pages. But although archived individual web pages are somewhat similar to newspapers—newspapers are published at a point in time, web pages are archived at a point in time (or close to)—if what is to be registered is a website, temporalities become more blurred. Although the point in time that a website was archived for the first time may be established, what follows after this point is a continuum, often without an end point, if the website is still being archived. Within this continuum, regular temporal subdivisions (as known from other media types) may not exist; the subdivisions may be haphazard, since they do not follow the producer's rhythm of publication, but the rhythm of archiving. Thus, temporal subdivisions may not be identical for all entities in a register.

It is evident that there are solutions or workarounds for establishing an overview of a selection of the archived web, but the point to be made here is that, because of the digitality of the archived web, such overviews—even with the most basic information—cannot be taken for granted, as they might be in other cases.

9.2.3 Evaluating Versions

When establishing the provenance or an overview of what should be studied, web historians may find it worthwhile to compare versions of a given archived web entity. As mentioned above, one of the aims of philology is the comparison of versions of manuscripts—for instance, mapping differences and similarities with a view to (possibly) identifying a shared "original" that has been copied in several manuscripts. In the same manner, web philology can compare versions of the archived web with a view to establishing how the online web in the past may have looked at a specific point in time (day, hour). And as with handwritten manuscripts, this cannot be determined with certainty, but only with varying degrees of probability.

Although web philology resembles philology generally, comparing versions of the old web is also different from comparing manuscripts, because the digitality of the archived web is different from that of texts written on parchment or paper. Therefore, these differences have to be mapped and taken into consideration.

First, the examination of variants of manuscripts mainly compares copies that were made at different points in time, whereas the archived web versions that are compared may originate from almost the same point in time. Although philology tends to compare backward in time, web philology tends to compare in simultaneity—that is, versions archived at close to the same point in time. This is also the reason that archived web versions cannot be considered copies of one another, as handwritten manuscripts may be, where one manuscript was written on the basis of another manuscript; instead, they are different "copies" of a lost original that none of them may be expected to be identical to.

Second, the dual nature of the online and of the archived web is different from that of handwritten manuscripts, for which only the visible text exists. The presence of a visible and a hidden text offers an array of possible ways to include the HTML code to help establish the relationship between versions, based on the development of a web philology toolbox to help access and compare web code. Even without including the HTML code as such, the displayed web page may partly indicate missing web elements by showing a placeholder, or revealing parts of the code when moused over. However, if the archived web sources come in the form of screenshots, files with individual web pages, or screen movies, the HTML code is not available, and therefore comparing this format of the archived web is closer to comparing manuscripts.

Third, in contrast to handwritten manuscripts, it is usually possible to date any archived web entity with a high degree of precision, but there is still a difference between the simple and the more complex forms of web archiving, since screenshots and the like may be very difficult to date, whereas the crawled web and the web retrieved via API come with precise time stamps.

Fourth, the archived web that is presented to researchers to evaluate has gone through a number of constructions—when archived, when preserved, and when made available—each of which in its way moves the available web away from what was initially online. What web philology aims to establish—the online web of the past—has been altered by the constructions of the archived web, which are different from changes and alterations in handwritten manuscripts, since the latter were usually made before the manuscripts were taken out of circulation and preserved, and not in the process of preservation.

Fifth, given the digital nature of the web, completely identical versions of a given web entity may actually exist in different web collections, but usually these are web elements (images, videos, etc.), as the bigger the web entity to be archived, the more time consuming it is to archive it, and the greater the risk of creating different versions.

Since the comparison of versions cannot determine how the online web of the past looked with certainty, but only with varying degrees of probability, the task of the web historian is to increase the degree of probability.

Although differences and similarities between existing versions may be compared, but not an original and the versions, it is still possible to outline a set of rules and guidelines to help make such comparisons more consistent, while still taking into account the digitality of the archived web. The simple guidelines outlined below primarily take the visible archived web as their point of departure, but the invisible web should be included as much as possible, to help.[2] However, at this time there are no easy-to-use tools that can show information about a given web element (for instance time stamp, shown by mouseover), or that can help automatically compare web pages (in total or in part), the closest being the previously mentioned Memento Time Travel.

To guide the evaluation of versions of the archived web, web historians may use the following six approaches, which may help to increase the reliability of what archived versions can tell about the online web of the past. The focus is on the web page, since it contains web elements, and pages may be interrelated to form a website, or be part of a web sphere. If the web pages being evaluated are shown in the Wayback Machine, the challenges related to embedded temporal inconsistency should be taken into consideration as a separate concern.

1. Provide as many versions as possible within the time range to be investigated: Several versions that point in the same direction may help substantiate a claim about how the online web of the past looked.

2. Use the most complete version as an "original": The more complete a version is, the better it can serve as an "original" to help guide comparisons. How (in)completeness is determined varies with the research question—for example, if images are to be studied, a version without images is incomplete, whereas for a study focusing exclusively on named entities, the same version may be considered complete.

3. Proximity in time and space: The closer the versions are to each other in time and in space (from the same collection or from another collection), the greater the possibility of establishing how the web entity looked when online.

4. Frequency of change of web elements: The more stable a given web element is supposed to be, the better the chance of it being identical across versions. This builds on an examination of the web elements on a web page, where some elements are considered stable with regard to position and content, such as logos, backgrounds, or menu items,

whereas others are supposed to have a high frequency of change, like news items or a social media feed.

5. Genre characteristics: The more stable the genre of the web page, the greater the probability that a given web element is identical over time. This approach is based on the assumption that some genres of web pages are supposed to be predominantly stable, such as pages on government institutions' websites, whereas others change rapidly, like web pages on news media websites. (This point is supported by an early study of the changeability of web pages that showed that material on the .com web domain changed much faster than material on .gov; cf. Cho & Garcia-Molina, 1999.)

6. Characteristics typical of the period: How a typical web page from a given period looked with regard to layout, navigational features, and specific web elements such as streaming video or flash, can help when evaluating how a given web element may have looked when online.

Each of the foregoing indicators may guide web historians evaluating a set of versions with a view to establishing how the online web probably looked in the past. In some cases, only one of them may be relevant, but they may also be combined, thus increasing the degree of probability of accurately determining how an element looked online, if they point to the same conclusion. For instance, the probability may be considered greater that a given web page actually looked the way one claims, if several versions have been provided, if one of these versions is close to complete, if the compared versions are close to each other in time and space, if the same stable web elements are present at the same position in several versions, and if genre characteristics and knowledge about the period's web characteristics point in the same direction.

9.2.4 Referencing

An integrated part of any historian's work is that of referencing the sources on which a study builds, with a view to identifying them unambiguously, thus enabling their possible retrieval. With the archived web this may be challenging, mainly because no established best practice exists yet. The following points may serve as a guide for how to reference the archived web.

If the archived web being used takes the form of screenshots, files with individual web pages, or screen movies that were found on the online web, either in a collection (e.g., one of the online web collections) or on the

World "Wild" Web, referencing should use the general standards for web references. However, apart from online web archives that do not usually change the URLs of their holdings, all other sorts of the archived online web are exposed to the high frequency of change of the web, and therefore such references may well be in vain. A solution is to try to find the material in a web archive, such as the Internet Archive, and reference it there.

If the archived web being used is the crawled web, in general the material should be referenced as precisely as possible. At a minimum, the information provided should include the name of the web archive or collection and the exact web address in the archive, as well as the date and the time of archiving, if such details exist.[3]

Finally, in the case of entire collections in the form of data sets, such as the GeoCities data set, or the "JISC UK Web Domain Dataset (1996–2013)," or researcher-generated corpora in general, as much information as possible should be added to the reference, including the site from which it was downloaded, its size, and other relevant data. In some cases, data sets also come with DOIs, as is the case with the JISC data set.

10   On the Edge of the Web

In his influential article, "Scarcity or Abundance? Preserving the Past in a Digital Era," historian Roy Rosenzweig perspicaciously identifies the paradox of digital media as a historical source. On the one hand, historians "need to act more immediately on preserving the digital present ...; they will be struggling with a scarcity, not an overabundance, of sources," but on the other hand, "the astonishingly rapid accumulation of digital data ... should make us consider that future historians may face information overload" (Rosenzweig, 2003, pp. 758, 738). This leads Rosenzweig to conclude: "Thus historians need to be thinking simultaneously about how to research, write, and teach in a world of unheard-of historical abundance and how to avoid a future of record scarcity" (Rosenzweig, 2003, p. 738). The web has existed for a little over 25 years, which in an internet world makes it at least a mature media form, if not an old one. During the web's lifetime, a number of applications and platforms initially existed on the edge of the web—phenomena such as email, newsgroups, online chat platforms, online social media, and obviously the telephone all predate the web—but at certain points in the web's history, they started to interact with the web and so to affect its development.

By and large the stories of the intersections between the web and the media forms that meander along its margins—and sometimes through its core—have not yet been written, although such histories are important, because they will shed new light on web history. One of the reasons for this gap may be that, although there is now an abundance of the old web in web archives, preserved sources from the edges of the web remain scarce. The lack of such sources, and by extension the lack of experience with these sources' digitality, make it challenging to write such stories. Therefore, to complete the picture of web history, some of the persistent holes in the digital source ecology are addressed in the following paragraphs, including how they interact with the web.[1]

10.1   Email, Newsgroups, and Online Chat Platforms

Before the advent of the web, born-digital media forms on the internet were usually separate software systems that had to be accessed through dedicated applications: one application for email, one for newsgroups, and one for online chat. From the user's point of view, the disadvantage of this archipelago of isolated software types was the lack of any possibility of bridging them. The web changed this, since these separate application types slowly moved to the web, where they became integrated with the web's communicative environment: webmail became widespread in the mid-1990s, newsgroups were integrated into the web, and web chat was enabled by web browsers. But despite the fact that the web integrated most of the previously separate application types, these also remained stand-alone applications, alongside the web. The intersections between these preweb forms and the web are important elements in web history, but it can be a challenge to write these web histories, because the source material is scarce.

Email was and is used for many types of communication, from correspondence between individuals and within organizations and companies, to newsletters, advertisements, and spam sent to a wide audience. But emails tend not to be collected and preserved in any systematic way, in either their preweb form or as webmail. In some cases, emails are private (and could thus be preserved in archives or folklore collections), and in other cases they may be considered public (and could then be preserved by libraries and web archives (as for webmail)).

Reports on preserving email have been published (e.g., Hampshire and Johnson, 2009; Prom, 2011), how to select emails has been debated (Cocciolo, 2016), and there are examples of email collections—for instance, the Danish Royal Library has established the MyArchive service, which facilitates the collection and preservation of emails. However, MyArchive is available only to writers, researchers, artists, and cultural personages, or private associations and institutions that have played a role in public cultural life, and an agreement must be made before emails may be deposited (see the MyArchive Service). Also, researcher-created collections exist (cf.

Paloque-Berges, 2017, p. 250). By and large, emails as the communicative glue that keeps societal life together in a great variety of fields are rarely preserved.

Newsgroups may have been preserved as part of some software systems, but not in any systematic way (Paloque-Berges, 2017, p. 230). When Usenet met the web in the early 1990s, a dual process started: the preweb newsgroups migrated to the web, and at the same time they were preserved on the web (Paloque-Berges, 2017, p. 232). However, as Paloque-Berges shows, moving Usenet to the web involves a continuous trade-off between Usenet's digital past and the changing present of the web, which results in a patchwork of overlapping and competing collections:

The main challenge regarding Usenet archives for historians and social scientists is their accessibility, fragmentation and non-exhaustivity: not only are there holes in the archives, a traditional historiographical problem, but there are also several collections with concurrent data and information systems. (Paloque-Berges, 2017, p. 248)

Online chat is a here-and-now medium and so has rarely been preserved, and in its web form online chat is not easily collected. Also, chat is often used for private communication, but when used for public communication, in many cases archiving institutions are entitled to collect it. As with email, online chat may have been preserved as part of research projects.

From a web historian's perspective, the challenge when working with forms of born-digital media that once existed at the edge of the web is that they have either rarely been collected and preserved, as is the case with email and online chat, or they may have been preserved, but the collections themselves may present challenges, as is the case with Usenet newsgroups. In any case, their specific digitality as reborn digital media may require the development of new methods to analyze them as such, and possibly to integrate them into the archived web.

10.2   Social Media

Social interaction in computer networks predates what are now called "social media," starting with bulletin board systems and newsgroups (Driscoll, 2016), but with advent of the web, other forms of online sociality emerged, such as the ones known as social media.

In general, the earliest forms of online social media were not preserved as such, so they have to be documented by the use of other types of sources, such as print media. But the same is also true of when social media met the web, at least in part. Social media websites may have been preserved in web archives, but for at least a decade, content on social media has presented some specific characteristics that have challenged its collection and preservation. Their content is updated much faster than that of websites in general, it is often fenced off, and social media are often highly integrated digital media environments (these three points are elaborated in greater detail by Brügger, 2018).

Most social media use some sort of status update, where news from its users is continuously presented in a feed, and these rapid updates are not easily archived, mainly because of their speed and the scale. Therefore, for the most part, only parts of them are archived by archiving institutions, often only those visible on the web page when opening it. A way of preserving updates in feeds is to retrieve them via the social media companies' API, but this is rarely done by large archiving institutions (see section 6.2).

Some parts of social media are fenced off because their communication is not public, but even when social media are publicly available in their online form, they may not have been archived. As shown by the example of the archived versions of Facebook in the Internet Archive, which came and went (section 4.6), social media may want to remain fenced off, despite the fact that they were initially public. Also, access via API may have been closed or changed (cf. section 6.5), and even an archived collection may not be made available, as is the case with the Twitter collection at the Library of Congress, which has not yet been made publicly accessible (Zimmer, 2015).

Finally, social media content is often distributed across the web, forming an integrated digital environment of embedded feeds, sharing, and streams. This presents challenges to collecting and preserving social media in their disseminated form, since even if feeds are preserved (e.g., via API), it may be difficult to patch together the various content streams and the websites in which they are embedded.

The web historian who wishes to write the history of when and how online social media met the web, and how they continued to develop as part of the web, may find this challenging.

10.3   Mobile Media

Telephones have a long history of their own, outside computer networks, but they have also become increasingly intertwined with digital networks, first when modems allowed for the establishment of networks, and later, when mobile devices became small computers in their own right, first as early mobile phones with a keyboard and text messaging, later with a camera, and finally as smartphones and tablet computers with touch screens, video cameras, and apps.

The development of the mobile phone is also intertwined with the web. On the one hand, the telephone developed independently of the web, when the landline telephone, as a speaking/listening device, was supplemented by a writing function (text messaging), and later became a full-scale computer in the form of the smartphone (cf. Goggin, 2018). On the other hand, the telephone met the web when smartphones started to include web browsers, and when content produced on smartphones could be embedded in websites—for instance, via social media. It is important to remember that although smartphones are usually associated with apps, they also come with web browsers. Thus, the web is part of the smartphone, along with apps and other application types, and still has the advantage of having an external hyperlink that can connect various websites, whereas apps are more like preweb applications, where no bridging between them is possible. Thus, smartphones provide a number of different application gateways to computer networks, of which the web is one.

Preserving content on a smartphone is challenging. Websites look different when viewed on a smartphone than when viewed on a laptop or desktop computer, and apps are mainly empty shells that are dependent on constant access to the server(s) from which they pull content. In some instances, app content may be archived by the use of an API from the content provider, but at the expense of the content not being presented as it looks on the mobile device. One of the only ways of preserving content on mobile devices, including the web, and the look and feel, is by taking screenshots or filming the screen, which obviously does not scale.

As with most other new media forms, the formative years of content on smartphones and tablet computers have not been preserved, and therefore studying the intersection between these media (let alone these media in themselves) and the web is not an easy task.

10.4   Web Histories on the Edge of the Web

Email, newsgroups, online chat, online social media, and the telephone existed before the web, and they have continued to develop more or less independently after the advent of the web. But they also intersect with the web in a number of ways: preweb applications, online social media, and the telephone were changed when they moved to or met the web, but the web was also changed, and it codeveloped as part of a mutual interplay. Therefore, these intersecting histories are relevant to web history.

If one wants to write the histories of these intertwined genealogies, it is important to preserve as much as possible of the original digital material to document these developments. However, email has been around for decades, but preservation is scattered and unsystematic, important parts of social media on the web continue to disappear, and no good solutions have yet been found for preserving content on mobile media. As with any other type of historical study, writing future histories of the edge of the web faces the challenge of having to make do with the sources available, but if no effort is made to move away from scarcity and closer to abundance, there will be very little to study.

If the necessary preserved copies of the above-mentioned digital phenomena become available, adequate theoretical and methodological frameworks are also needed to unlock and understand their digitalities as reborn digital media in their own right. Their specific digitality may require new methods to be developed to analyze them, and possibly to integrate them with instances of the archived web, particularly in cases where they share part of their digitality with the archived web. How should emails, newsgroups, and chat be studied? What about social media, on the web and on other platforms? And how can apps and mobile media in general be studied? A possible starting point could be to reevaluate the framework that has been presented in this book, in light of the digitalities of the digital phenomena on the edge of the web.

11 Conclusion—the Future of Web History

◆

As the preceding chapters have demonstrated, a critical investigation of the web in its archived form is crucial, if one wants to use the archived web as a scholarly source to support web history research. The argument that all digital media are not digital in the same way, just because they are digital, means that each digital medium has its specific digitality. When this approach is used as the point of departure for understanding the archived web, it becomes apparent that in many ways the archived web is clearly distinct from both digitized and born-digital media forms, such as the online web.

11.1 The Archived Web—Transformations of the Online Web

Although the online and the archived web are different, it should not be forgotten that they are also closely entwined, since the online web and its three relatively fixed features—the two textual layers and its fragmented and hyperlinked nature—are the starting point from which the digitality of the archived web emerges. Therefore, the online web constitutes the origin of the archived web, but this point of origin is transformed and reconstructed in various ways until it eventually reaches scholars who can use it in their research. The online web was transformed when collected, depending on which forms and strategies were used, and the collected web was transformed when preserved and made available, depending on the various choices made by the archiving actor. When confronted with these constructions and transformations, it is then up to researchers to adopt a critical approach and identify, evaluate, and untangle all the different choices, constraints, and possibilities embedded in the different stages of the chain of web archiving, prior to the research project in question. When this is in place, the last transformation may get underway, namely, that of the researcher transforming the archived web into a research object—through search, selection, and corpus creation—that may ultimately be analyzed.

If the specific nature of the archived web is not acknowledged at the outset, the scholar risks unreflectively using the archived web as a source. Either she is not fully abreast of a true web history source criticism, where the validity of the research claims may not be fully supported, or she risks failing to unlock the full potential of this new source type—for example, by including the hidden code of the archived web as one element of study among others.

Most historians, even those who work with digital history, probably lack expertise in dealing critically with the archived web. The scholarly use of the archived web as a source must be based on rigorous web archive criticism, an academic "web archive literacy," so to speak—that is, a systematic, critical, and reflective approach that helps to identify both the pitfalls and the advantages of the archived web. The core of web archive literacy should be an awareness of the myriad transformations the archived web has undergone, from when it first appeared online until it became available for use in a research project, as well as the ability to assess the consequences of these transformations for scholarly practices.

11.2   Outline of an Agenda for the Future of Web History

Although researchers may still be grappling with how to implement web archive literacy, things move on in the online world, and new questions and tasks already loom on the horizon of future web history. Some of these challenges revolve around changes in the object of study—the digital media, including the web—whereas others are more intrinsic to research practices, and still others relate to the structures that support the communities in which web history research is embedded.

11.2.1   Changes in the Object of Study

As mentioned in chapter 10, the present object of study—the web, online as well as archived—has been supplemented by new digital media forms, such as apps and mobile media. Therefore, web researchers must try to keep pace with these new developments, first, by discussing the extent to which these phenomena on the edge of the web may be considered "the web," second, by debating how they may be collected and preserved, preferably in collaboration with archiving institutions, and third, by developing and testing suitably rigorous analytical methods in line with the digitalities of these types of material.

11.2.2   Challenges Intrinsic to Research Practices

As to the issues inherent in research practices, some of the fundamental steps that may help scholars understand the archived web have been taken, but a couple of things have been neglected. First, it is imperative that more—and more relevant—documentation be provided by the organizations that handle the archived web, in particular about the provenance of the archived material. In many cases the information is already there, such as in automatically generated metadata files like crawl logs, but it needs to be made available and unwrapped alongside the crawled web content itself. The documentation should be context-sensitive with respect to the research process, which means that some sort of documentation is needed before a research project starts, such as general information about the collection, whereas other sorts of information are needed during the various phases of the process.[1]

Second, more could be done to develop and sustain research infrastructures, to support the scholarly use of the archived web as a source, and to support its expansion. Much has happened on the technical and curatorial sides of web archiving, but the development of structures to support researchers' use of the material is lagging behind, especially when it comes to the use of the collections by scholars unfamiliar with digital media. Research infrastructures should include easy access to documentation, as mentioned above, among other things by providing transnational access to metadata for collections not freely available online, easy-to-use software tools to help search, select, and extract what must be studied, and work spaces with some fundamental web history tools. In particular, it is important to have dedicated work spaces within the boundaries of collections that are not freely available online. Finally, research infrastructures should also include the establishment of research data management policies and structures to support these—that is, structures that can handle the movement of data (or derived data) through the entire lifecycle of the research process.

Third, it is time for reflection on ethical issues related to web history research to appear on the agenda. Today there is so much material in web collections—and so many different types of material—that we, as researchers, are able to do more than we may want to—for instance, utterances that might have been kept private in nondigital media environments are now being made public. The general question here is how to strike a balance between the need to present research to society, and the imperative of not harming individuals or groups. How this balance is to be negotiated is not yet clear, but it is important to start debating how already existing practices in historical research fit the digitality of the archived web.

11.2.3   Structures to Support Web History Communities

The structures that support the communities in which web history research is embedded may also be developed further. In 2010 I concluded the edited volume *Web History* (Brügger, 2010) with an epilogue titled "The Future of Web History." As outlined in that brief contribution, much needed to be done as of 2010 to establish the emerging field of web history. Looking back on the list of proposals today, it is impressive how much has actually been accomplished since then. Lots of groundbreaking research has been done (see chapter 4 and the list of references), the number of web archiving actors has grown, and today web archiving is accomplished in a great variety of ways. Transnational web history research projects have slowly begun to be conducted, collaborative archiving initiatives have taken place, close collaborations between web archives and researchers have grown, and international conferences have been established by the two main international communities—the IIPC's annual General Assembly Open Day, and the biannual conference organized by RESAW (RESearcher use of the Archived Web). An international peer-reviewed journal has also been founded (*Internet Histories*), and the field has become mature enough for its first comprehensive reference work to appear (Brügger & Milligan, 2018).

To promote web history research in the digital age, there is still work to do to help the research community expand. Since the web has been such an integral digital element around the world for over two decades, one may expect young scholars to soon start automatically including the archived web as a source in their research. However, although they may be "digital natives" who have grown up in a digital media environment, they are not born with an understanding of the reborn web. Also, until now, the use of the archived web has primarily involved internet and new media studies or has been the province of a few dedicated historians with an interest in these fields. However, there is a need to reach out to historians in general, and to researchers from any other discipline where the archived web could be relevant and useful.

A major task for all stakeholders involved in working with the archived web is to use the accomplishments to date as a foundation for the next steps in web history: to propagate a commitment to web archive literacy among younger generations of researchers, and among researchers who do not consider themselves web historians but could benefit from access to the archived web. The preceding points may seem the most obvious and urgent items on the agenda of future web history. But just as the agenda I sketched in my 2010 epilogue has had to be modified to reflect the changing times, to a great extent it is up to the two new communities of scholars just mentioned—young scholars and web historians to come—to set an agenda for the next 25 years of web history research.

Notes

Introduction

1. A brief analysis of the changes in whitehouse.gov's issue list in 2001, 2006, and 2008 can be found in Rogers (2013, pp. 70–71).

2. For an overview of other examples, see Winters (2017a).

3. Previous versions of whitehouse.gov have been preserved by several institutions, including the End of Term Web Archive that has been collecting the US Government websites at the end of presidential administrations since 2008 (http://eotarchive.cdlib.org). The British Conservative Party's political speeches were archived by the British Library, and the social media post by a Russian may be found in the Internet Archive. In the *TechCrunch* article from which the quote above about whitehouse.gov is taken, a screenshot of whitehouse.gov from the Obama period taken from the Internet Archive is used as documentation.

4. See the historical studies of the internet by Abbate (2000); Hauben and Hauben (1997); Naughton (2002, 2012); Poole (2005); Goggin and McLelland (2017); Brügger et al. (2017). Histories of the web are provided by Brügger (2010, 2016c, 2017c); Burns and Brügger (2012); Brügger and Schroeder (2017); Brügger and Laursen (2018); Brügger and Milligan (2018).

Chapter 1: Doing Web History in the Digital Age

1. William G. Thomas III maintains that the Virginia Center for Digital History, founded in 1997–1998, was probably the first to use this term (Cohen et al., 2008, p. 453). Weller distinguishes between "digital history" and "historians more generally in the digital age" (Weller, 2013, p. 3); the former is a recognized subfield of history with a strong emphasis on digital tools and methods, whereas the latter comprises historians "who engage with online and digital resources ... but whose primary concern is not technological development in the field" (Weller, 2013, p. 4).

2. An overview of the discussions prompted by this book may be found at http://historymanifesto.cambridge.org/media. Other important contributions to the discussion of born- and reborn digital sources include works by Milligan (2013), Putnam (2016), and Graham et al. (2016) (the latter publication introduces a number of tools and approaches to studying big historical data).

3. The web, considered as a historical source, is mentioned once in the book in relation to the attacks on the US on September 11, 2001 (Cohen & Rosenzweig, 2006, p. 161). In the 2003 article "Scarcity or Abundance? Preserving the Past in a Digital Era," Rosenzweig also mentions the Internet Archive as "an extraordinarily valuable resource" (Rosenzweig, 2003, p. 751), and some characteristics of this type of material are briefly identified (various forms of incompleteness, its dynamic and hyperlinked nature) (p. 742).

4. Other examples of web history as history with the web and as history of the web may be found in chapter 4.

Chapter 2: The Digital and the Web

1. Ernst also uses the term *digitality* in passing, without elaborating on it (Ernst, 2013, p. 82).

2. For a general history of the computer, see Ceruzzi (1998).

3. Bits may also be represented in formats other than electricity, such as punch cards and paper tape.

4. Conceptualizing the digital as an alphabet is not very widespread. Berry and Fagerjord also note that "as the programmer types, the code is translated into an alphabet with only two characters, famously known as 0s and 1s" (Berry & Fagerjord, 2017, p. 90). Ernst briefly mentions "the unexpected return of writing in the form of the most minimal alphabet conceivable (0/1)," without, however, elaborating on this insight (Ernst, 2013, p. 88). Evens (2012) emphasizes the binary 0/1 as the point of departure for the development of digital artifacts and culture, but considers 0/1 as numbers.

5. *Text* is understood in a broad sense, possibly including all semiotic systems, not only written text.

6. To designate the specific nature of a medium as medium and the specific nature of a text as text, I have elsewhere used the terms *mediacy* and *textuality*, inspired by the "medium theory" tradition in media studies that aims to identify a set of "relatively fixed features" (Meyrowitz, 1994, p. 50), and textual linguistics (Vater, 1994; Beaugrande & Dressler, 1996), based on the argument that any text has a specific way of establishing itself as a coherent unit that can make sense to a reader, listener, viewer, or user (see also Brügger, 2002, pp. 43–52; Brügger, 2009, pp. 119–125).

7. The materiality and embeddedness of the digital in material artifacts are also emphasized by Berry and Fagerjord (2017, pp. 90–91).

8. Finnemann also maintains that any use of computers is grounded in an invisible yet operational alphabet (Finnemann, 1999, p. 148). See also Zundert and Andrews's (2017) discussion of various forms of digital texts.

9. Insisting on the nexus between the material and the digital has affinities for the approaches adopted by Hayles (2002), Kirschenbaum (2008), and Owens (2018), among others. And the duality of the digital text resonates with Chun's idea that software cannot be reduced to the software code as such, but must also be seen as executed software (e.g., Chun, 2011, pp. 19–29).

10. The term *born-digital* is also used by Berry (2012, p. 4), Kirschenbaum (2013), and Jones (2014, p. 6). Rogers (2013) also distinguish between digitized and what he terms "natively digital" material (Rogers, 2013, pp. 14–15, 19).

11. For a detailed comparison of the archived web, and digitized newspapers and broadcast media, see Brügger (2016a, 2011). Rogers (2013) also thematizes to what extent the methods used are a function of the material being either "natively digital" or digitized (Rogers, 2013, pp. 19–38).

12. One could also argue that the web browser is a constitutive part of the web; see Brügger (2017a). For a history of web browsers see Elmer (2002) and Weber (2018).

13. Although the word *visible* is used here, it covers any sort of experienced semiotic system (as opposed to the nonexperienced text), be it visual or auditory. Sound is important on the web (cf. Jensen & Helles, 2007; Morris, 2018), but to avoid repeating "visual or auditory," "visible" is used for all semiotic systems throughout the rest of the book.

14. In the following, the term HTML is used as an umbrella term to cover the different versions of HTML as well as XHTML, which has been in use since 2000 as a combination of HTML and the general-purpose markup language XML.

15. This is obviously a very simple setup, but although things are more complicated with dynamic web pages, this is basically what happens.

16. Several hundred types of files exist; see the list at https://www.iana.org/assignments/media-types/media-types.xhtml.

17. The latter is what Tim Berners-Lee, the inventor of the web, called a "hotspot" in the initial proposal for the World Wide Web (Berners-Lee, 1989, p. 10).

18. See Brügger (2017a) for a prehistory of the hyperlink, as well as Helmond (2018) and Barnet (2013, 2018) for different approaches to the history of the hyperlink.

Chapter 3: Five Analytical Web Strata

1. What is understood by semantic, formal, and physical performative is explained in more detail in Brügger (2009, pp. 121–122) and Brügger (2010, pp. 19–24).

2. Cf. Brügger (2009, p. 121) about the difference between morphological and syntactic analysis.

3. The visible web strata may also be studied at scale, but not in their online form, and not without adding some extra layers of processing. As shown in section 4.1.4, this is the case with a study of the use of written text on web pages, based on screenshots of web pages that are then processed by the use of image recognition software (Cocciolo, 2015).

4. Although some workarounds to this problem exist, like visualizations of millions of images on "image walls" or similar that enable zooming in/out, this is only a partial solution. It is still not possible to closely read millions of images, even if they are presented on an image wall, but patterns may be recognized (cf. also Manovich, 2012).

Chapter 4: Cases of Web History

1. The examples have been selected on the basis of what is probably the bulk of the existing web history literature, some 250 publications, including books, journal articles, book chapters, and conference papers. The cases have been selected because they use the archived web as a source and because each illustrates a specific concern of the theoretical framework. Although the examples show the range and variety of web historiography, they are not representative of the literature as such.

2. The "JISC UK Web Domain Dataset (1996–2013)" was created in a partnership between the UK Web Archive, the Internet Archive, and JISC, and it contains all the web material from the Internet Archive hosted on the .uk web domain from 1996 to 2013 (for documentation about the data set, see data.webarchive.org.uk/opendata/ukwa.ds.2). Secondary data sets, such as Geoindex and Host Link Graph, are made available by the UK Web Archive, based on this data set. The JISC data set is also the data set that the UK Web Archive's search engine, SHINE, queries (SHINE was developed as part of the research project "Big UK Domain Data for the Arts and Humanities (BUDDAH)" (2014–2015)).

3. robots.txt is a standard file used by websites to communicate with web robots, including web crawlers, if a website does not want to be crawled.

4. This collection is still available at the Library of Congress.

Chapter 5: Archiving the Web

1. Some of the often unacknowledged practices and processes involved in web archiving are revealed by Schafer et al. (2016). In a similar vein, Rogers talks about "the dominant approaches to web archiving and their in-built historiographies" (Rogers, 2018, n.p.). How web archivists work with and shape the web archive has also been studied (see Huc-Hepher, 2015, and Ogden et al., 2017).

2. For example, Rosenzweig (2003), Owens (2018), and Rinehart and Ippolito (2014) provide insightful and relevant overviews of the preservation of digital media, digital preservation, and the conservation of new media art, respectively, but do not provide an in-depth understanding of the (archived) web.

3. It may also be argued that the personalization of the web to a specific user, be it an individual or an archiving institution (based on previous user behavior, browser settings, etc.), adds another layer to the representation. But this aspect is not taken into account in the following sections, because strictly speaking it concerns what it was possible to archive, and not the web archiving process as such.

4. Not only is web crawling the most widespread archiving form in most major (inter)national archiving projects, it has also been setting the agenda for most of the literature about web archiving.

5. The aim of the comparison with digitized collections is not to characterize the complexity and variety of such collections, but to establish a contrast that makes the digitality of the archived web clearer. A more detailed analysis of digitized collections in their own right should take the complexities and variations of these collections into account.

6. Brügger uses the phrase "document of the web" to indicate that "the object of analysis, the Internet, constitutes a raw material which is already mediated, and in its archiving a new document *of it* is created" (Brügger, 2005, p. 30).

7. Histories of web archiving and web archives are found in Brügger (2011, pp. 29–32), Webster (2017b), Koerbin (2017), and Laursen and Møldrup-Dalum (2017); the latter two focus mainly on web crawling and national web archives. Also see Webster (2018) and Rogers (2018).

8. For a brief discussion of archiving with screen movies, see Brügger (2005, pp. 49–53).

9. It is worth noting that what was previously termed a *screencast* (chapter 4) is not the same as a screen movie. A screen movie is any movie made by filming what occurs on the screen to preserve this, whereas a screencast is a movie made of individual screenshots (i.e., still images) and combined with a voice-over to trace the development of a web page. However, the screencast may also be composed of screen movies.

10. *Web crawling* and *web harvesting* are often used synonymously. For introductions to web crawling, see Masanès (2006) and Brown (2006).

11. The ARC compression file format created by the Internet Archive was used between 1996 and 2009, whereas the WARC format (Web ARChive), a revision of the ARC format, has been the common standard for storing crawled web material since 2009.

12. An overview of the possible settings in crawling software used in macro web archiving may be found at https://webarchive.jira.com/wiki/spaces/Heritrix/overview (for the Heritrix web crawler).

13. See Weltevrede (2016, pp. 25–52) on the use of the API.

14. The use of the API for academic purposes is discussed by Lomborg and Bechmann (2014) and for Twitter in particular by Driscoll and Walker (2014) and Kumar et al. (2015).

15. The problem of updating is discussed in more detail in relation to the front pages of newspaper websites by Falkenberg (2006, pp. 8–9). See also Ainsworth et al. (2015).

Chapter 6: The Web of the Past—Where to Find What?

1. "List of Web Archiving Initiatives" (n.d.) and IIPC members (n.d.) provide extensive overviews of existing web collections, in some cases indicating archiving forms and strategies used.

2. However, in many cases, collections made by the Internet Archive's Archive-It may be accessed in three ways: through the website of the subscriber, through the Archive-It website (see archive-it.org), and in the Internet Archive itself.

3. For the cultural history of web archives, see the contributions by Webster (2017b, 2018), Koerbin (2017), and Laursen and Møldrup-Dalum (2017).

4. A detailed overview of this type of web archive may be found in Truman (2016).

5. The first iteration of the Wayback Machine was launched in October 2001. The metaphors related to the name "Wayback Machine" are discussed by Ankerson (2015).

6. An overview of some of the most important of these collections may be found in Truman (2016, pp. 67–68).

7. Also see the previously mentioned web archeology project to restore the digital city of Amsterdam (de Haan, 2016; Alberts et al., 2017).

Chapter 7: The Web of the Past as a Historical Source

1. A pilot test of versions archived on the same date and as close in time as possible in different archives performed in 2007 highlights the differences between versions (cf. Brügger, 2008, p. 161).

2. See Milligan (2016, pp. 85–89) for a discussion of metadata and the archived web.

3. The Memento Time Travel feature (timetravel.mementoweb.org) shows how a given web page may be patched together in bits and pieces originating from different web archives and from different points in time to create a copy as close as possible to how the web page may have looked at some specific time in the past. This clearly illustrates what happens when the Wayback Machine patches together a web page from fragments from the same web archive (see the reflections on Memento in Winters, 2017b). The Memento protocol is introduced by Nelson and van de Sompel (2018).

4. It is possible to prevent the Wayback software from working this way, but many (if not all) web archives using the Wayback software do not do this, as the result of a trade-off between showing either as complete a version as possible, or a temporally consistent copy.

5. This function may also be disabled when a web archive sets up the Wayback software.

Chapter 8: Scholarly Use of the Archived Web

1. Lin et al. (2017) use a process model for studies of web archives called the FAAV cycle with the following phases: filter, analyze, aggregate, visualize. Visualization of the results is not included in the present context because in many cases this takes place in programs that are not part of the web collection, such as Gephi, for network graphs. Therefore, what is relevant is how the corpus of the collection may be prepared to fit into visualization software (for an overview of web history and visualization, see Joque, 2018).

2. Brügger (2013) and Stevenson and Ben-David (2018) provide an overview of the historical network analysis of hyperlinks.

3. Because of the size of the Internet Archive, only front pages are indexed.

Chapter 9: Toward a Source Criticism of the Archived Web

1. Such collaborations have already been established in several countries, such as bursaries to support researcher use of web archives (e.g., by the BUDDAH project in the UK, and by the Portuguese Web Archive), workshops targeted at researchers

(e.g., Atelier DL Web INA in France, NetLab in Denmark), and more formal collaborations, such as the editorial board of the Danish Netarkivet (appointed by the Ministry of Culture), where researchers also have a seat.

2. The following rules and guidelines for web philology are further developed by Brügger (2008, pp. 165–170).

3. Initiatives to standardize references to the archived web have emerged. See for instance Nyvang et al. (2017), who argue for the establishment of "a transparent persistent web material identification" for material in web archives. This would consist of the name of the web archive, time of archiving, archived URL, and content coverage—for example, "specification: Web archive: archive.org, archiving time: 2016–04–20 18:21:47 UTC, archived URI: http://resaw.eu, content coverage: webpage"—and would include a PWID URI (persistent web identifier) (Nyvang et al., 2017, pp. 6–7).

Chapter 10: On the Edge of the Web

1. Obviously, a number of other digital ephemera exist that are also rarely preserved, such as listservs, text messages, and instant messages.

Chapter 11: Conclusion—the Future of Web History

1. Maemura et al. (2018) constitutes one of the first attempts to address these issues related to provenance.

References

Abbate, J. (2000). *Inventing the Internet*. Cambridge, MA: MIT Press.

Ackland, R., & Evans, A. (2017). Using the web to examine the evolution of the abortion debate in Australia, 2005–2015. In N. Brügger & R. Schroeder (Eds.), *The web as history* (pp. 159–189). London: UCL Press.

Agata, T., Miyata, Y., Ishita, E., Ikeuchi, A., & Ueda, S. (2014). Life span of web pages: A survey of 10 million pages collected in 2001. *Proceedings of the 14th ACM/IEEE-CS Joint Conference on Digital Libraries* (pp. 463–464). Piscataway, NJ: IEEE Press.

Ainsworth, S. G., Nelson, M. L., & van de Sompel, H. (2015). Only one out of five archived web pages existed as presented. *Proceedings of the 26th ACM Conference on Hypertext & Social Media, HT '15*, pp. 257–266. doi:10.1145/2700171.2791044.

Alberts, G., Went, M., & Jansma, R. (2017). Archaeology of the Amsterdam digital city: Why digital data are dynamic and should be treated accordingly. *Internet Histories*, 1(1–2), 146–159.

Allen-Robertson, J. (2017). The materiality of digital media: The hard disk drive, phonograph, magnetic tape and optical media in technical close-up. *New Media & Society*, 19(3), 455–470.

Ankerson, M. S. (2015, June 8–10). *Web history as time travel: Digital nostalgia & collaborative filtering in public engagement with the Internet Archive's WayBack Machine*. Paper presented at the conference titled Web Archives as Scholarly Sources: Issues, Practices and Perspectives, Aarhus.

Arnold, J. H. (2000). *History: A very short introduction*. Oxford: Oxford University Press.

Aust, R. (2014, December 3). *Online reactions to institutional crises: BBC Online and the aftermath of Jimmy Savile*. Paper presented at the conference titled Web Archives as Big Data, London. http://sas-space.sas.ac.uk/id/eprint/6100.

Barnet, B. (2013). *Memory machines: The evolution of hypertext*. London: Anthem Press.

Barnet, B. (2018, forthcoming). Hypertext before the web—or, what the web could have been. In N. Brügger & I. Milligan (Eds.), *The SAGE handbook of web history* (n.p.). London: SAGE.

Barry, M. (2017). Untangling the threads: Public discourse on the early web. In N. Brügger (Ed.), *Web 25: Histories from the first 25 years of the World Wide Web* (pp. 57–76). New York: Peter Lang.

Beaudouin, V., Pehlivan, Z., & Stirling, P. (2018, forthcoming). Exploring the memory of the First World War using web archives: Web graphs seen from different angles. In N. Brügger & I. Milligan (Eds.), *The SAGE handbook of web history* (n.p.). London: SAGE.

de Beaugrande, R., & Dressler, W. (1996). *Introduction to text linguistics*. Essex: Longman.

Ben-David, A. (2016). What does the web remember of its deleted past? An archival reconstruction of the former Yugoslav top-level domain. *New Media & Society*, 18(7), 1103–1119.

Berners-Lee, T. (1989). Information management: A proposal. https://www.w3.org/History/1989/proposal.html.

Berry, D. M. (2012). Introduction: Understanding the digital humanities. In D. M. Berry (Ed.), *Understanding digital humanities* (pp. 1–20). New York: Palgrave Macmillan.

Berry, D. M., & Fagerjord, A. (2017). *Digital humanities: Knowledge and critique in a digital age*. Cambridge: Polity.

Brown, A. (2006). *Archiving websites: A practical guide for information management professionals*. London: Facet.

Brügger, N. (2002). Theoretical reflections on media and media history. In N. Brügger & S. Kolstrup (Eds.), *Media history: Theories, methods, analysis* (pp. 33–66). Aarhus: Aarhus University Press.

Brügger, N. (2005). *Archiving websites: General considerations and strategies*. Aarhus: Centre for Internet Studies.

Brügger, N. (2008). The archived website and website philology: A new type of historical document? *Nordicom Review*, 29(2), 155–175.

Brügger, N. (2009). Website history and the website as an object of study. *New Media & Society*, 11(1–2), 115–132.

Brügger, N. (Ed.). (2010). *Web history*. New York: Peter Lang.

Brügger, N. (2011). Digital history and a register of websites: An old practice with new implications. In D. W. Park, N. W. Jankowski, & S. Jones (Eds.), *The long history of new media: Technology, historiography, and contextualizing newness* (pp. 283–298). New York: Peter Lang.

Brügger, N. (2013). Historical network analysis of the web. *Social Science Computer Review, 31*(3), 306–321. doi:10.1177/0894439312454267.

Brügger, N. (2015). A brief history of Facebook as a media text: The development of an empty structure. *First Monday, 20*(5), n.p.

Brügger, N. (2016a). Digital humanities in the 21st century: Digital material as a driving force. *Digital Humanities Quarterly, 10*(2), n.p.

Brügger, N. (2016b). Introduction: The web's first 25 years. *New Media & Society, 18*(7), 1059–1065.

Brügger, N. (2016c). The web's first 25 years [Special issue]. *New Media & Society, 18*(7).

Brügger, N. (2017a). Connecting textual segments: A brief history of the web hyperlink. In N. Brügger (Ed.), *Web 25: Histories from the first 25 years of the World Wide Web* (pp. 3–28). New York: Peter Lang.

Brügger, N. (2017b). Probing a nation's web domain: A new approach to web history and a new kind of historical source. In G. Goggin & M. McLelland (Eds.), *The Routledge companion to global internet histories* (pp. 61–73). New York: Routledge.

Brügger, N. (Ed.) (2017c). *Web 25: Histories from the first 25 years of the World Wide Web.* New York: Peter Lang.

Brügger, N. (2018). Web history and social media. In J. Burgess, A. Marwick, & T. Poell (Eds.), *The SAGE handbook of social media* (pp. 196–212). London: SAGE.

Brügger, N., Goggin, G., Milligan, I., & Schafer, V. (2017). Internet Histories [Special issue]. *Internet Histories, 1*(1–2).

Brügger, N., & Laursen, D. (2018). *The historical web and digital humanities: The case of national web domains.* Abingdon: Routledge.

Brügger, N., Laursen, D., & Nielsen, J. (2017). Exploring the domain names of the Danish web. In N. Brügger & R. Schroeder (Eds.), *The web as history* (pp. 62–80). London: UCL Press.

Brügger, N., & Milligan, I. (Eds.). (2018). *The SAGE handbook of web history.* London: Sage.

Brügger, N., & Schroeder, R. (Eds.). (2017). *The web as history: Using web archives to understand the past and the present.* London: UCL Press.

Burns, M., & Brügger, N. (Eds.). (2012). *Histories of public service broadcasters on the web.* New York: Peter Lang.

Ceruzzi, P. E. (1998). *A history of modern computing*. Cambridge, MA: MIT Press.

Chakraborty, A., & Nanni, F. (2017). The changing digital faces of science museums: A diachronic analysis of museum websites. In N. Brügger (Ed.), *Web 25: Histories from the first 25 years of the World Wide Web* (pp. 157–172). New York: Peter Lang.

Chambers, S., & Mechant, P. (2018, forthcoming). Towards a national web in a federated country: A Belgian case study. In N. Brügger & D. Laursen (Eds.), *The historical web and digital humanities: The case of national web domains* (n.p.). Abingdon: Routledge.

Cho, J., & Garcia-Molina, H. (1999). The evolution of the web and implications for an incremental crawler. *Proceedings of the 26th International Conference on Very Large Databases*.

Chun, W. H. K. (2011). *Programmed visions: Software and memory*. Cambridge, MA: MIT Press.

Cocciolo, A. (2015). The rise and fall of text on the web: A quantitative study of web archives. *Information research*, 20(3), n.p.

Cocciolo, A. (2016). Email as cultural heritage resource: Appraisal solutions from an art museum context. *Records Management Journal*, 26(1), 68–82. doi:10.1108/RMJ-04-2015-0014.

Cohen, D. J., Frisch, M., Gallagher, P., Mintz, S., Sword, K., Taylor, A. M., et al. (2008). The promise of digital history. *Journal of American History*, 95(2), 452–491.

Cohen, D. J., & Rosenzweig, R. (2006). *Digital history: A guide to gathering, preserving, and presenting the past on the web*. Philadelphia: University of Pennsylvania Press.

Cooke, L. (2005). A visual convergence of print, television, and the internet: Charting 40 years of design change in news presentation. *New Media & Society*, 7(1), 22–46.

Cordell, R. (2017). "Q i-jtb the raven": Taking dirty OCR seriously. *Book History, 20*, 188–225. doi:https://doi.org/10.1353/bh.2017.0006.

Cowls, J. (2017). Cultures of the UK web. In N. Brügger & R. Schroeder (Eds.), *The web as history* (pp. 220–237). London: UCL Press.

Cowls, J., & Bright, J. (2017). International hyperlinks in online news media. In N. Brügger & R. Schroeder (Eds.), *The web as history* (pp. 101–116). London: UCL Press.

Craven, T. (2002). What is the title of a web page? A study of webography practice. *Information Research*, 7(3). http://InformationR.net/ir/7-3/paper130.html.

Deken, J. M. (2017). The web's first "killer app": SLAC National Accelerator Laboratory's World Wide Web site 1991–1993. In N. Brügger (Ed.), *Web 25: Histories from the first 25 years of the World Wide Web* (pp. 43–56). New York: Peter Lang.

Dougherty, M., Meyer, E. T., Madsen, C., Heuvel, C. D., Thomas, A., & Wyatt, S. (2010). *Researcher engagement with web archives: State of the art.* London: JISC.

Driscoll, K. (2016). Social media's dial-up roots. *IEEE Spectrum*, 53(11). doi:10.1109/MSPEC.2016.7607028.

Driscoll, K., & Walker, S. (2014). Working within a black box: Transparency in the collection and production of Big Twitter Data. *International Journal of Communication*, 8, 1745–1764.

Elmer, G. (2002). The case of web browser cookies: Enabling/disabling convenience and relevance on the web. In G. Elmer (Ed.), *Critical perspectives on the internet* (pp. 49–62). Lanham: Rowman & Littlefield.

Engholm, I. (2002). Digital style history: The development of graphic design on the internet. *Digital Creativity*, 13(4), 193–211.

Engholm, I. (2003). *WWW's designhistorie: Website udviklingen i et genre- og stilperspektiv (WWW's design history: Website development from the perspective of genre and style).* Copenhagen: IT University of Copenhagen Press.

Ernst, W. (2013). *Digital memory and the archive.* Minneapolis: University of Minnesota Press.

Etherington, D. (2017, January 20). The official White House website has dropped any mention of climate change. *TechCrunch*. https://techcrunch.com/2017/01/20/the-official-white-house-website-has-dropped-any-mention-of-climate-change.

Evens, A. (2012). Web 2.0 and the ontology of the digital. *Digital Humanities Quarterly*, 6(2), n.p.

Falkenberg, V. (2006, October 19–20). *Metodologiske utfordringer ved arkivering av nettaviser.* Paper presented at the Medieforskerlagets Årskonferanse, Bergen.

Finnemann, N. O. (1999). Modernity modernised: The cultural impact of computerisation. In P. A. Mayer (Ed.), *Computer, media and communication* (pp. 141–159). Oxford: Oxford University Press.

Foot, K., & Schneider, S. (2006). *Web campaigning.* Cambridge, MA: MIT Press.

Foot, K., & Schneider, S. (2010). Object-oriented web historiography. In N. Brügger (Ed.), *Web history* (pp. 61–79). New York: Peter Lang.

Gebeil, S. (2015a). *La fabrique numérique des mémoires de l'immigration maghrébine sur le web français (1999–2014).* Aix-Marseille: Ecole Doctorale Espaces, Cultures, Sociétés (Aix-en-Provence).

Gebeil, S. (2015b). Le web, nouvel espace de mobilisation des mémoires marginales: Les mémoires de l'immigration maghrébine sur l'internet français (2000–2013). *Cahiers Mémoire et Politique, 2.*

Goggin, G. (2018, forthcoming). Emergence of the mobile web. In N. Brügger & I. Milligan (Eds.), *The SAGE handbook of web history* (n.p.). London: SAGE.

Goggin, G., & McLelland, M. (Eds.). (2017). *The Routledge companion to global internet histories*. New York: Routledge.

Graham, S., Milligan, I., & Weingart, S. (2016). *Exploring big historical data: The historian's macroscope*. London: Imperial College Press.

Guldi, J., & Armitage, D. (2014). *The history manifesto*. Cambridge: Cambridge University Press.

de Haan, T. (2016). Project "The Digital City Revives": A case study of web archaeology. In *Proceedings of iPres 2016*. Bern: iPres

Halavais, A. (2018, forthcoming). How search shaped and was shaped by the web. In N. Brügger & I. Milligan (Eds.), *The SAGE handbook of web history* (n.p.). London: SAGE.

Hale, S. A., Blank, G., & Alexander, V. D. (2017). Live *versus* archive: Comparing a web archive to a population of web pages. In N. Brügger & R. Schroeder (Eds.), *The web as history* (pp. 45–61). London: UCL Press.

Hampshire, E., & Johnson, V. (2009). The digital world and the future of historical research. *Twentieth Century British History*, 20(3), 396–414.

Hauben, M., & Hauben, R. (1997). *Netizens: On the history and impact of Usenet and the internet*. Los Alamitos, CA: IEEE Computer Society Press.

Hayles, N. K. (2002). *Writing machines*. Cambridge, MA: MIT Press.

Helmond, A. (2017). Historical website ecology: Analyzing past states of the web using archived source code. In N. Brügger (Ed.), *Web 25: Histories from the first 25 years of the World Wide Web* (pp. 139–155). New York: Peter Lang.

Helmond, A. (2018, forthcoming). A historiography of the hyperlink: Periodizing the web through the changing role of the hyperlink. In N. Brügger & I. Milligan (Eds.), *The SAGE handbook of web history* (n.p.). London: SAGE.

Hockey, S. (2000). *Electronic texts in the humanities*. Oxford: Oxford University Press.

Hockey, S. (2004). The history of humanities computing. In S. Schreibman, R. Siemens, & J. Unsworth (Eds.), *A companion to digital humanities* (pp. 3–19). Malden, MA: Blackwell.

Hockx-Yu, H. (2015, June 8–10). *The unknown aspects of web archives*. Paper presented at the conference titled Web Archives as Scholarly Sources: Issues, Practices and Perspectives, Aarhus.

Hofheinz, A. (2010). A history of Allah.com. In N. Brügger (Ed.), *Web history* (pp. 105–135). New York: Peter Lang.

Huc-Hepher, S. (2015). Big web data, small focus: An ethnosemiotic approach to culturally themed selective web archiving. *Big Data & Society*, 2(2), 1–15. doi:10.1177/2053951715595823.

IIPC members. (n.d.). http://netpreserve.org/about-us/members.

Jackson, A. (2015). *Ten years of the UK web archive: What have we saved?* Paper presented at the 2015 IIPC GA, Palo Alto.

Jensen, K. B., & Helles, R. (2007). The silent web: A qualitative study of sound as information and communication in websites. In M. Consalvo & C. Haythornthwaite (Eds.), *Internet research annual* (Vol. 4, pp. 183–194). New York: Peter Lang.

Jessen, I. B. (2010). The aesthetics of web advertising: Methodological implications for the study of genre development. In N. Brügger (Ed.), *Web history* (pp. 257–277). New York: Peter Lang.

Jones, S. E. (2014). *The emergence of the digital humanities*. New York: Routledge.

Joque, J. (2018, forthcoming). Visualizing historical web data. In N. Brügger & I. Milligan (Eds.), *The SAGE handbook of web history* (n.p.). London: SAGE.

Karampelas, G. (2014, October 29). Stanford Libraries unearths the earliest U.S. website. *Stanford Report*. http://news.stanford.edu/news/2014/october/slac-libraries-wayback-102914.html.

Kimpton, M., & Ubois, J. (2006). Year-by-year: From an archive of the internet to an archive on the internet. In J. Masanes (Ed.), *Web archiving* (pp. 201–212). Berlin: Springer.

Kirschenbaum, M. (2008). *Mechanisms: New media and the forensic imagination*. Cambridge, MA: MIT Press.

Kirschenbaum, M. (2013). The .txtual condition: Digital humanities, born-digital archives, and the future literary. *Digital Humanities Quarterly*, 7(1), n.p.

Koerbin, P. (2017). Revisiting the World Wide Web as artefact: Case studies in archiving small data for the National Library of Australia's PANDORA Archive. In N. Brügger (Ed.), *Web 25: Histories from the first 25 years of the World Wide Web* (pp. 191–206). New York: Peter Lang.

Krol, E. (1992). *The whole Internet: User's guide and catalog*. Sebastopol, CA: O'Reilly & Associates.

Kumar, S., Morstatter, F., & Liu, H. (2015). Analysing Twitter data. In Y. Mejova, I. Weber, & M. W. Macy (Eds.), *Twitter: A digital socioscope* (pp. 21–51). Cambridge: Cambridge University Press.

Laursen, D., & Møldrup-Dalum, P. (2017). Looking back, looking forward: 10 years of development to collect, preserve, and access the Danish web. In N. Brügger (Ed.),

Web 25: Histories from the first 25 years of the World Wide Web (pp. 207–227). New York: Peter Lang.

Li, X., & Zhunag, L. (2007). Cultural values in internet advertising: A longitudinal study of the banner ads of the top U.S. web sites. *Southwestern Mass Communication Journal*, 23(1), 57–72.

Lin, J., Milligan, I., Wiebe, J., & Zhou, A. (2017). Warcbase: Scalable analytics infrastructure for exploring web archives. *Journal on Computing and Cultural Heritage, 10(4), n.p.*

List of web archiving initiatives. (n.d.). https://en.wikipedia.org/wiki/List_of_Web _archiving_initiatives.

Lomborg, S., & Bechmann, A. (2014). Using APIs for data collection on social media. *Information Society*, 30(4), 256–265. doi:10.1080/01972243.2014.915276.

Lubar, S. (1999). Information culture and the archival record. *American Archivist*, 62, 10–22.

Maemura, E., Worby, N., Milligan, I., & Becker, C. (2018, forthcoming). If these crawls could talk: Studying and documenting web archives provenance. *Journal of the Association for Information Science and Technology*.

Manovich, L. (2012). How to compare one million images? In D. M. Berry (Ed.), *Understanding digital humanities* (pp. 249–278). New York: Palgrave Macmillan.

Manovich, L. (2013). *Software takes command*. New York: Bloomsbury.

Masanès, J. (Ed.). (2006). *Web archiving*. Berlin: Springer.

Mataly, J. (2013). *The three truths of Margaret Thatcher: Creating and analysing archival artefacts*. Master's thesis, University of Amsterdam.

Mayer-Schönberger, V. (2009). *Delete: The virtue of forgetting in the digital age*. Princeton, NJ: Princeton University Press.

Mayer-Schönberger, V., & Cukier, K. (2013). *Big data: A revolution that will transform how we live, work, and think*. New York: Houghton Mifflin Harcourt.

McLelland, M. (2017). Early challenges to multilingualism on the internet: The case of Han character-based scripts. *Internet Histories*, 1(1–2), 119–128.

McMichael, A., Rosenzweig, R., & O'Malley, M. (1996). Historians and the web: A beginner's guide. *Perspectives Online*, 34(1). http://www.historians.org/perspectives/ issues/1996/9601/9601COM3.CFM.

Meyrowitz, J. (1994). Medium theory. In D. Crowley & D. Mitchell (Eds.), *Communication theory today* (pp. 50–77). Cambridge: Polity.

Milligan, I. (2012). Mining the "internet graveyard": Rethinking the historians' toolkit. *Journal of the Canadian Historical Association/Revue de la Société historique du Canada*, 23(2), 21–64. doi:10.7202/1015788ar.

Milligan, I. (2013). Illusionary order: Online databases, optical character recognition, and Canadian history, 1997–2010. *Canadian Historical Review*, 94(4), 540–569.

Milligan, I. (2016). Lost in the infinite archive: The promise and pitfalls of web archives. *International Journal of Humanities and Arts Computing*, 10(1), 78–94. doi:10.3366/ijhac.2016.0161.

Milligan, I. (2017). Welcome to the web: The online community of GeoCities during the early years of the World Wide Web. In N. Brügger & R. Schroeder (Eds.), *The web as history* (pp. 137–158). London: UCL Press.

Moretti, F. (2000). Conjectures on world literature. *New Left Review*, 1(January), 56–58.

Morris, J. W. (2018, forthcoming). Hearing the past: The sonic web from MIDI to music streaming. In N. Brügger & I. Milligan (Eds.), *The SAGE handbook of web history* (n.p.). London: SAGE.

Mufson, S., & Dennis, B. (2017, January 20). References to climate change disappear from White House website. *Washington Post*. https://www.washingtonpost.com/local/2017/live-updates/politics/live-coverage-of-trumps-inauguration/references-to-climate-change-disappear-from-white-house-website/?utm_term=.5a6aac130b1f.

Musso, M., & Merletti, F. (2016). This is the future: A reconstruction of the UK business web space (1996–2001). *New Media & Society*, 18(7), 1120–1142.

The MyArchive Service. (n.d.). http://www.kb.dk/en/nb/samling/myarchive/index.html.

Nagy, A. (2012). 23 ancient web sites that are still alive. *Gizmodo.com*. https://gizmodo.com/5960831/23-ancient-web-sites-that-are-still-alive.

Nanni, F. (2017). Reconstructing a website's lost past: Methodological issues concerning the history of Unibo.it. *Digital Humanities Quarterly*, 11(2), n.p.

Natale, S., & Bory, P. (2017). Constructing the biographies of the web: An examination of the narratives and myths around the web's history. In N. Brügger (Ed.), *Web 25: Histories from the first 25 years of the World Wide Web* (pp. 29–42). New York: Peter Lang.

Naughton, J. (2002). *A brief history of the future: The origins of the internet*. London: Phoenix.

Naughton, J. (2012). *From Gutenberg to Zuckerberg: What you really need to know about the internet*. London: Quercus.

Naylor, J. S., & Sanchez, C. A. (2017, April 25). Smartphone display size influences attitudes toward information consumed on small devices. *Social Science Computer Review*, online first. doi:10.1177/0894439317704161.

Nelson, M. L., & Sompel, H. van de. (2018, forthcoming). Adding the dimension of time to HTTP. In N. Brügger & I. Milligan (Eds.), *The SAGE handbook of web history* (n.p.). London: SAGE.

Nolan, S. (2017). Born outside the newsroom: The creation of the Age Online. In N. Brügger (Ed.), *Web 25: Histories from the first 25 years of the World Wide Web* (pp. 107–122). New York: Peter Lang.

Ntoulas, A., Cho, J., & Olston, C. (2004, May 17–22). *What's new on the web? The evolution of the web from a search engine perspective.* Paper presented at the conference titled *WWW2004*, New York.

Nyvang, C., Kromann, T. H., & Zierau, E. (2017, June 14–15). *Capturing the web at large: A critique of current web referencing practices.* Paper presented at the Second RESAW Conference, London.

Ogden, J., Halford, S., & Carr, L. (2017, June 25–28). *Observing web archives: The case for an ethnographic study of web archiving.* Paper presented at the conference titled WebSci '17, Troy, NY.

Owens, T. (2018, forthcoming). *The theory and craft of digital preservation: An introduction.* Baltimore: Johns Hopkins University Press.

Paloque-Berges, C. (2017). Usenet as a web archive: Multi-layered archives of computer-mediated communication. In N. Brügger (Ed.), *Web 25: Histories from the first 25 years of the World Wide Web* (pp. 229–252). New York: Peter Lang.

Park, H. W., Barnett, G. A., & Chung, C. J. (2011). Structural changes in the 2003–2009 global hyperlink network. *Global Networks*, 11(4), 522–542.

Poole, H. W. (Ed.). (2005). *The internet: A historical encyclopedia.* Santa Barbara, CA: ABC/Clio.

Prom, C. J. (2011). *Preserving email.* Heslington: Digital Preservation Coalition. 10.7207/twr11-01.

Putnam, L. (2016). The transnational and the text-searchable: Digitized sources and the shadows they cast. *American Historical Review*, 121(2), 377–402.

Raffal, H. (2014, December 3). *The online development of the Ministry of Defence (MoD) and Armed Forces.* Paper presented at the conference titled Web Archives as Big Data, London. http://sas-space.sas.ac.uk/6250.

Rinehart, R., & Ippolito, J. (2014). *Re-collection: Art, new media, and social memory.* Cambridge, MA: MIT Press.

Rogers, R. (2013). *Digital methods.* Cambridge, MA: MIT Press.

Rogers, R. (2017). Doing Web history with the Internet Archive: Screencast documentaries. *Internet Histories*, 1(1–2), 160–172.

Rogers, R. (2018, forthcoming). Periodizing web archiving: Biographical, event-based, national and autobiographical traditions. In N. Brügger & I. Milligan (Eds.), *The SAGE handbook of web history* (n.p.). London: SAGE.

Rosenzweig, R. (2003). Scarcity or abundance? Preserving the past in a digital era. *American Historical Review*, 108(June), 735–762.

Schafer, V., Musiani, F., & Borelli, M. (2016). Negotiating the web of the past: Web archiving, governance and STS. *French Journal for Media Research*, 6, n.p. http://frenchjournalformediaresearch.com/lodel/index.php?id=952.

Schneider, S. M., & Foot, K. A. (2004). The Web as an Object of Study. *New Media & Society*, 6(1), 114–122.

Stevenson, M. (2016). Rethinking the participatory web: A history of HotWired's "new publishing paradigm," 1994–1997. *New Media & Society*, 18(7), 1331–1346.

Stevenson, M., & Ben-David, A. (2018, forthcoming). Network analysis for web history. In N. Brügger & I. Milligan (Eds.), *The SAGE handbook of web history* (n.p.). London: SAGE.

Terras, M. (2012). Digitization and digital resources in the humanities. In C. Warwick, M. Terras, & J. Nyhan (Eds.), *Digital humanities in practice* (pp. 47–70). London: UCL/Facet Publishing.

Teszelszky, K. (2018, forthcoming). Web archiving before the web archive: How to reconstruct and save the Dutch national web using historical methods. In N. Brügger & D. Laursen (Eds.), *The historical web and digital humanities: The case of national web domains* (n.p.). Abingdon: Routledge.

Thomas, W. G., III. (2004). Computing and the historical imagination. In S. Schreibman, R. Siemens, & J. Unsworth (Eds.), *A companion to digital humanities* (pp. 56–68). Oxford: Blackwell.

Thorsen, E. (2010). BBC News Online: A brief history of past and present. In N. Brügger (Ed.), *Web history* (pp. 213–232). New York: Peter Lang.

Tosh, J. (2006). *The pursuit of history: Aims, methods and new directions in the study of modern history*. Harlow: Pearson Longsman.

Truman, G. (2016). *Web archiving environmental scan*. Harvard Library Report. http://nrs.harvard.edu/urn-3:HUL.InstRepos:2565831.

Udell, J. (2005a). Heavy Metal Umlaut. http://jonudell.net/udell/gems/umlaut/umlaut.html.

Udell, J. (2005b). Heavy Metal Umlaut: The making of the movie. Boston: O'Reilly. http://archive.oreilly.com/pub/a/network/2005/02/07/primetime.html.

Vater, H. (1994). *Einführung in die Textlinguistik*. Munich: Fink.

Weber, M. (2018, forthcoming). Browsers and browser wars. In N. Brügger & I. Milligan (Eds.), *The SAGE handbook of web history* (n.p.). London: SAGE.

Weber, M. S. (2012). Newspapers and the long-term implications of hyperlinking. *Journal of Computer-Mediated Communication*, 17, 187–201.

Webster, P. (2017a). Religious discourse in the archived web: Rowan Williams, Archbishop of Canterbury, and the sharia law controversy of 2008. In N. Brügger & R. Schroeder (Eds.), *The web as history* (pp. 190–203). London: UCL Press.

Webster, P. (2017b). Users, technologies, organisations: Towards a cultural history of world web archiving. In N. Brügger (Ed.), *Web 25: Histories from the first 25 years of the World Wide Web* (pp. 175–190). New York: Peter Lang.

Webster, P. (2018, forthcoming). Religion and web history. In N. Brügger & I. Milligan (Eds.), *The SAGE handbook of web history* (n.p.). London: SAGE.

Weller, T. (2013). Introduction: History in the digital age. In T. Weller (Ed.), *History in the digital age* (pp. 1–19). Abingdon: Routledge.

Weltevrede, E. (2016). *Repurposing digital methods: The research affordances of platforms and engines*. Amsterdam: Amsterdam School for Cultural Analysis (ASCA).

Weltevrede, E., & Helmond, A. (2012). Where do bloggers blog? Platform transitions within the historical Dutch blogosphere. *First Monday*, 17(2), n.p.

Wiggins, R. (1996). The mysterious disappearance of the White House speech archive: A pioneering application of technology vanishes. *First Monday*, 1(2), n.p.

Wiggins, R. (2001). The unnoticed presidential transition: Whither Whitehouse. gov? *First Monday*, 6(1), n.p.

Winters, J. (2017a). Breaking in to the mainstream: Demonstrating the value of internet (and web) histories. *Internet Histories*, 1(1–2), 173–179.

Winters, J. (2017b). Coda: Web archives for humanities research—some reflections. In N. Brügger & R. Schroeder (Eds.), *The web as history* (pp. 238–248). London: UCL Press.

Winters, J. (2018, forthcoming). Negotiating the archives of UK web space. In N. Brügger & D. Laursen (Eds.), *The historical web and digital humanities: The case of national web domains* (n.p.). Abingdon: Routledge.

Zimmer, M. (2015). The Twitter archive at the Library of Congress: Challenges for information practice and information policy. *First Monday*, 20(7), n.p. http://firstmonday.org/ojs/index.php/fm/article/view/5619/4653.

Zundert, J. J. van, & Andrews, T. L. (2017). Qu'est-ce qu'un texte numérique?—A new rationale for the digital representation of text. *Digital Scholarship in the Humanities*, 32(suppl. 2), pp. 78–88. doi: https://doi.org/10.1093/llc/fqx039.

Index

0/1 (binary notation), 17–21

Abortion, 59–60
Academic Torrents, 97
.ac.uk, 37
Age Online, 55
Alexa, 54
Algorithm, 46, 67–68
allah.com, 54
Antwerp City Archives, 94
API (Application Programming
    Interface), 59–60, 82–83, 89–90, 98–
    99, 109–110, 117, 134–135, 138–139,
    152–153
App, 22, 23, 83, 153
Application Programming Interface. *See*
    API
ARC, file, 82, 111, 131
Archive, 77
Archive-It, 91, 93, 94, 96
Archive-It Research Services (ARS), 93
Archive Team, 97–98
Archivethe.net, 91
Archiving unit, 87, 129
Armed forces, 57–121
ArtBase, 96
Artifact, 5, 17–22, 73, 77, 138,
    162n4(ch2), 163n7
ASCII code, 21, 22
Audio, 29, 45–46, 77, 81, 88
Audiovisual media, 3, 21
Australia, 59–60

Banner ad, 42–45
BBC, 52, 56–57
Belgium, 64
Berners-Lee, Tim, 66, 100, 163n17
Bibliothèque Nationale de France (BNF),
    51–52, 60–61
Big data analysis, 124, 133–134
Big UK Domain Data for the Arts
    and Humanities (BUDDAH), 52–53,
    164n2(ch4), 167n1(ch9)
Bit, 18
Bitmap, 26, 126
Blog, 63, 100
Blogosphere, 63
BNF. *See* Bibliothèque Nationale de
    France
Born-digital, 5–6, 12–13, 21–23, 74
British Library, 161n3
Browser, 4, 23–30, 31, 33–35, 37–40, 66,
    69–70, 80, 82–83, 89, 96, 100, 115–
    116, 150, 153, 163n12
BUDDAH. *See* Big UK Domain Data for
    the Arts and Humanities
Bush, George, 1–2

ccTLD (country code top level domain),
    37, 63, 64–65, 76, 94
CD-ROM, 22, 83
CDX, 113, 131, 133, 141
Chat, online, 150–151
Clinton, Bill, 1–2, 101
CMS, 37, 83

Columbia University Libraries, 97
.com, 37, 76, 147
Common Crawl, 93
Conservative Party (British), 2
Cookie, 29, 44, 69–70
Corpus creation, 122, 133, 134, 156
Country code top level domain. *See* ccTLD (country code top level domain)
Crawl log, 82, 112, 121, 131, 132, 141, 157
Cross-collection studies, 135
Current Events in Africa Web Archive (CEAWA), 94

Denmark, 63–64, 65, 76, 94, 101
Digital history, 11–16
Digital humanities, 17
Digitality, 5–6, 17, 19–21
  duality of, 19–21
  of the online web, 23–30, 74, 86
Digital Methods Initiative, 50
Digitized, 5–6, 12–13, 21–23, 26, 28, 30, 75, 77, 85–89, 105–106, 108–109, 112–113, 122, 128, 137–138, 142–144
.dk, 37, 76, 84–85
dk-hostmaster, 76
Documentation, 91, 93, 95, 98, 109, 157
Dutch blogosphere, 63, 133
Dutch Web Archive, 94–95
Dynamics of updating, 87–88, 106

Elbaz, Gil, 93
Email, 150–151
Ephemerality, 51

Facebook, 22, 68–69, 92, 98
Film, 77
.fr, 37, 84–85
Fragmentation of the web. *See* Web, fragmentation of the
France, 51, 61, 167–168n1(ch9)

Generic Top Level Domain. *See* gTLD
GeoCities, 58–59
GeoCities Snapshot, 58–59, 97–98, 148
Geoindex, 164
Giant bucket, 127, 138
Global web, 66–67
Google, 50–51, 59, 67, 69
  and the politics of tabs, 50–51
.gov, 37, 76, 147
.gov.uk, 37, 94
Graphics, 20, 24, 27, 28, 33, 89
gTLD (generic top level domain), 37

Handwritten manuscripts, 21, 33, 72, 113, 137, 144–147
Heritrix, 82
Hidden, 6, 20–21, 24–31, 33, 35–40, 41, 55–61, 63–66, 69–70, 71, 89–90, 126, 127–134, 134–135, 145
History
  of the web, 5, 15, 42–51, 53–59, 61–66, 66–68, 71
  with the web, 5, 15, 51–54, 59–61, 69, 71–72
History web, 14–16
Host Link Graph, 60, 164n2(ch4)
HotWired, 55
HTML (HyperText Markup Language), 23–30, 46, 82, 83
HTTP (HyperText Transfer Protocol), 23
Human Rights Web Archive @ Columbia University, 97
Hyperlink, 28–30, 56–57, 60–61, 64–65, 86, 90, 107–109, 114, 122–124
  network, 56–57, 59–60, 63, 66–67, 122–124

Icelandic Web Archive, 95
Image, 6, 18, 20–22, 24, 26–35, 37–39, 46–48, 57–59, 80–81, 88–100, 109–111, 112–115, 121, 125–126, 130–131, 146
Image recognition, 126, 164n3

INA. *See* Institut National de l'Audiovisuel
info.cern.ch, 99
Institut National de l'Audiovisuel (INA), 51–52, 94–96, 167n1
Internet Archive, 43, 45, 46–47, 49–51, 53, 54, 55, 56, 58, 60, 62, 64, 65, 68–69, 70, 76, 78, 92–93, 98, 101, 114–116, 127, 132, 148
Internet Explorer, 69–70
Internet Memory Research, 91
.it, 53
Italy, 53–54

JISC UK Web Domain Dataset (1996–2013), 52-53, 55-58, 60, 65, 69, 95, 148, 164n2

Kahle, Brewster, 92

Layers of the web. *See* Web, layers of the
Library, 77–78
Library of Congress, 62, 95, 142, 152
LGA file (Longitudinal Graph Analysis), 112–113, 131, 132, 133
Longitudinal Graph Analysis file. *See* LGA

Macro web archiving, 79, 81, 84–85
Media artifact, 5, 19–21
Mediacy, 162n6
Memento protocol, 167n3(ch7)
Memento Time Travel, 128, 141, 146, 167n3(ch7)
Metadata, 25, 82, 95, 112–113, 140–142
Micro web archiving, 79–80, 85
Ministry of Defence (UK), 57
Mobile media, 153
Mobile phone, 153
Modem, 153
Mosaic, 96, 100
MyArchive, 150

National web, 63–66, 106
National web archives, 84–85, 93–96
Netarkivet, 65, 76, 94–96, 127, 167n1
Netherlands, 63, 64
NetLab, 167n1
Netscape, 69–70
Network analysis. *See* Hyperlink, network
News, 49–50, 56–57, 60
Newsgroups, 150–151
Newspaper, 22–23, 26–28, 30, 38, 49–50, 60, 77, 85–89, 105–106, 108–109, 112–113, 128, 142–144
New York Times, 70, 133
nytimes.com, 70, 133

Obama, Barack, 1–2
OCR (Optical Character Recognition), 22, 26, 112, 126
oldweb.today, 70, 96
Online web. *See* Web, online
Optical Character Recognition. *See* OCR

PADICAT, 94
PANDORA, 94–95, 127, 142
Philology. *See* Web philology
Podcast, 45
Portuguese Web Archive, 78, 94, 127, 132, 167n1(ch9)
Print media, 49–50, 83–84, 101
Provenance, 5, 21, 22, 77, 100, 137, 140–142, 157

Radio, 18, 21, 22, 31, 45, 77, 85–89, 112, 128, 142–144
Reborn digital, 5–6, 12–13, 21–23, 74
Referencing, 147–148
Registry, 142–144
Research data management, 139, 157
Research infrastructure, 157
Rhizome, 96
robots.txt, 53, 68–69, 92, 94, 164n3(ch4)

Savile, Jimmy, 52
Science museums, 55
Screen cast documentary, 50–51
Screen movie, 81, 89–90, 109–111, 125–127, 135, 140, 147–148
Screen shot, 80–81, 88, 89–90, 106, 109–111, 125–127, 135, 140, 147–148
Second Life, 85, 95
Search, 50–51, 67, 127–128, 130, 131–132
secondlife.com, 85
Seed-list, 82, 112, 121, 131, 132, 141
Seed URLs, 82
SHINE, 65, 164n2(ch4)
SLAC National Accelerator Laboratory, 99
Smartphone, 153
Social media, 82–83, 98–99, 134, 151–152
Sound, 18, 22, 24, 26, 27, 33, 35, 45–46, 105
Source criticism, 137–138, 139–147
Stanford University Libraries, 99
Stanford Web Archive Portal, 99
Streaming, 24, 45, 88, 147

Telephone, 153
Television, 49–50, 84, 101
Text, 5, 19–21
Text messaging, 153
Textuality, 22, 26, 69, 162n6
Thatcher, Margaret, 69, 125
Tracker technology, 29, 40, 70
TripAdvisor, 55–56
tripadvisor.co.uk, 55–56
Trump, Donald, 1
Tweet ID Datasets, 99
Twitter, 22, 98, 152

UCLA Online Campaign Literature Archive, 96
.uk, 37, 60, 64, 65, 69, 84–85, 96

UK (United Kingdom), 64, 94
UK Conservative Party. See Conservative Party (British)
UK Web Archive, 69, 76, 78, 94–98, 127, 129
Ukraine, 2
unibo.it, 53–54, 86, 135
United Kingdom. See UK
United States., 1–2, 46–47, 60, 62–63, 97
University of Bologna, 53–54
URI (Uniform resource identifier). See URL
URL (Uniform resource locator), 23, 57, 81–82, 127, 142–143

Version, 74, 104, 107, 109, 113–114, 120–122, 124, 135, 137, 139, 140, 144–147
Visible, 6, 16, 20, 24–35, 37–40, 41, 42–51, 54–55, 57–59, 61–63, 66, 68–70, 71, 89–90, 125–126, 127–131, 134, 135, 145
Visualization, 167n1(ch8)
VOSON, 59–60

WANE file (Web Archive Named Entities), 113, 131, 132
WARC, 58, 82, 111, 131, 133
WAT file (Web Archive Transformation), 61, 113, 131, 132
Wayback Machine, 43, 45, 47, 49–51, 53, 55, 56, 57, 58–59, 92–93, 95, 98, 112, 114–117, 127–134, 141, 143, 146
Web ad. See Banner ad
Web archive literacy, 156–159
Web Archive Named Entities file. See WANE file (Web Archive Named Entities file)
Web Archive Norway, 95
Web Archive Transformation file. See WAT file (Web Archive Transformation file)

Web archiving, 6, 73–90
  forms, 78, 85–89
  strategies, 78, 84–85, 85–89
Web
  audio, 45
  crawler, 53, 60, 82, 114, 141
  element, 33, 35, 42–47, 68–70
  fragmentation of the, 26–28, 90
  harvesting, 166n10
  history, 4–5, 14–16, 41–72
  layers of the, 24–26, 89
  lifetime of, 75–77
  online, 2–9, 16, 17, 23–30, 31, 73–90,
    100–101, 104, 107–110, 113–117,
    121–123, 137, 144–148
  page, 33–34, 37, 47–51, 70
  page design, 48–50, 57
  radio, 45
  sound, 45–46
  sphere, 34–35, 37, 59–66, 70
  strata, 6, 32–40, 41–72, 108
  as a whole, 35, 37, 66–68, 69–80
Web crawling, 81–82, 86, 88, 89–90,
    106, 109–110, 111–117, 127–134,
    135, 138–139, 140–141, 148
Web Design Museum, 96
Webmuseum.dk, 96
Web philology, 122, 137, 144–147
Webrary, 77–78
Webrecorder, 82
webrecorder.io, 82
Website, 34, 37, 51–59, 68–70
What you see is what you can get, 89,
    109–110, 125–126
What you can get is what may be
    assembled, 109–110, 111, 127–
    135
White House, 1, 75
whitehouse.gov, 1, 5, 75, 101
Wired, 55
World War 1, 60–61
World "Wild" Web, 48, 66, 68–69, 100–
    101, 105, 110, 140, 148

Written text, 27, 46, 47, 69, 120, 125,
    126, 133, 162n5, 164n3(ch3)

Yahoo, 65–67, 97–98
.yu, 64–65
Yugoslavia, 64–65

Zenodo, 97
Zero/one. See 0/1 (binary notation)

Printed in the United States
by Baker & Taylor Publisher Services